How to Make a House a Home

Clarkson
Potter/
Publishers
New York

How to Make a House a Home

Creating a Purposeful, Personal Space

Ariel Kaye

Illustrations by **Babeth Lafon** / Illustration Division

For my mother, Cathy, and
daughter, Lou James

CONTENTS

Welcome Home

Your home should tell a story of who you are. Like the clothes you wear, your home's design is an outward expression and point of pride worthy of your attention, thoughtfulness, and time.

First, what is the difference between a house and a home? A house is a structure filled with pieces that have function—a table, a bed, a chair. It is a roof and walls that together form rooms, and the corridors that run in between to connect them. But a home is something else. A home captures a feeling the moment you walk through the door. A home is the combined essence of colors, shapes, and textures that evoke emotions in you and in others.

At its most basic, a house provides shelter, while a home is so much more.

A home **welcomes, nurtures,** and gives you a **sense of security**
A home feels **authentic, distinctive,** and **personal**
A home inspires, keeps you **curious, invites rituals,** and **tells your story**
A home engages your **mind, body, spirit,** and **senses**
The idea of "home" is more than a place; it's a sanctuary that gives a feeling of belonging.

About Me

My passion for a warm, inviting, beautiful home started early. Growing up, my parents' home was the place where friends and family gathered. I learned from my mother and father to value what my home expressed and how it made people feel. They created a place where people in our lives wanted to come by and stay for a visit or a meal.

When I moved into my first apartment, I embraced the notion that it was a space I could make my own. The ideas and aesthetic were mine alone—not my family's and not a collective idea with a roommate or partner. I considered each room and then each area within the rooms, seeking an easy comfort. I relished the minutes—okay, maybe hours—spent tinkering, finding ways to improve or deepen my connection with my home. And I always wanted it to welcome others.

Over time, I realized that my home, more than any single possession, spoke to who I was. I cared less about being noticed for a new handbag, preferring a conversation sparked by a piece of vintage art hung on my wall. My friends started to come in looking for what I had added or changed that week, whether something substantial, like a new wooden bookshelf, or little things that added character, like rearranging the items on my coffee table. My home was a canvas where I could experiment with new ideas of who I wanted to be.

Since then, my focus on my home has evolved with me, and has remained a constant creative outlet. My interest became my passion. Soon, friends were asking me for help with *their* spaces. They knew I wasn't a professional designer, but they were seeking the sense of home I'd fostered in my tiny, cramped apartment. I relished the opportunity to guide a girlfriend or my sister through flea markets and furniture stores selecting hanging shelves, an upholstered storage bench, or a cozy chair. I would rummage through their drawers and discover a perfect scarf to frame and place over the bed.

I quickly realized I was gaining more enjoyment from these informal design projects than from my professional work in advertising. I had unlocked a new aspect of my creativity—and I wanted more! Ultimately, I was inspired to create Parachute, a company where we now make modern bedding, bath, rugs, and tabletop and other decor for a more comfortable home and at-ease lifestyle.

The name Parachute is inspired by the movement of the fabric when you make your bed—the billowing sheet floating through the air and gracefully landing. I wanted the brand to capture that effortlessness and beauty. It was a simple idea in the beginning. We spend one-third of our lives sleeping, and our sheets and towels touch our skin every day. The fabrics in our home should be stylish as they take care of us and provide warmth, comfort, and a sense of serenity.

I believe this philosophy applies to our personal spaces as well. At Parachute, this overarching concept is our foundation. Our collective purpose revolves around our vision to make your house your home. The same passion and philosophy that inspired me to create Parachute inspired me to write this book.

My home began as an address on a street in a neighborhood. But it's much more than that now. My home is a state of mind. Where I land. The physical structure I depend upon for a feeling of comfort and safety, of acceptance, of permission to let go and to be myself. Countless times I have thought, "I can't wait to be home." Home is where I laugh, cry, love, mend, mess up the kitchen, sleep in, stay up late, and curl up.

My underlying principles remained constant as I switched coasts from New York City to Los Angeles, moved into a bigger space with my husband, got married, and started a family. When we first moved in, we had a house. It was a bungalow with walls and floors and a roof. Right

103

away I knew the closets were too small but the backyard was ideal for gatherings. How would my husband and I—sharing each room and bringing our own identities—fit together and make this place work for both of us, day in and day out? How would we make the house into a home?

I began, as this book begins, with finding the flow and I moved from there. Step-by-step, I went through the process described within these pages. Just like with a good friend, my home and I had to build a relationship. We ultimately had to "get" each other.

And of course, once I got our home to a place where I could say, "Done!" our life changed. I was pregnant. We would be welcoming a baby, which triggered the beginning of a new journey to discover what this home means to each of us individually and as a family.

Now I laugh when I remember that I ever thought we were "done." Just as I hope to continually evolve and grow, my home is never finished. What feels right today may feel questionable down the road. It's why my big-ticket items are simple and neutral, so they can be more permanent as I alter and modify other elements.

My perspective on home is similar to describing a mood. We have quiet moments when we want to kick back. Then we can quickly transition from resting to being energetic. We crave inspiration and aspiration. We are curious and dynamic. These characteristics add up to an intriguing person—and to a flexible, vibrant home that changes with us from dawn to dusk. When I have one more touch to add to the sofa or a wall, I wonder, "How does this reflect a part of me?" Our home reflects who we are at our harmonious best.

Thank you for joining me. Whether you're updating your bedroom or redoing your living room or taking on the whole house, enjoy the journey.

About This Book

With all this promise of what a home can be, let's explore the possibilities. This is not a decorating book in the typical sense. You won't find design decrees. Instead, I offer concepts, suggestions, and tips to help you create a space that speaks to your lifestyle and fulfills you. While the notion of "home" can seem intangible, this book is about discovering what home means to you, and empowering you to envision and execute that space.

I have distilled the principles that organically make a house a home, and am fascinated by them—they are what guides the organization here. I begin with identifying the overarching purposes for different spaces and bringing in components of styling that maximize the benefits you are seeking. You will find questions that guide you to set directions for moving forward with valuable changes, and inspiration to get you there. Throughout, you'll find helpful ideas and examples that will take any and every room to the next level.

Remember, houses come in all shapes and sizes. Creating a home is not about the amount of space you have; it's what you choose to do with your space that makes it reflective of you.

Ready to Start?

I've been there. Tackling a redesign can seem overwhelming. Even setting up a single room can be daunting. But think about it this way: You have an opportunity to build a space that feeds your body, mind, and soul, and truly expresses your point of view. Before picking out paint colors or moving the sofa, sit somewhere comfortable. Set your intentions and gather some inspiration.

First, Reflect and Prioritize

Do you have an overall wish list for your home? Do you want to maximize space? Add color? Tidy up? Make a list—and be honest with yourself. Put a star by the idea that you keep thinking about. Start there. If you can only take on your bedroom right now, let that be enough. Or if the idea is to make your space light and bright, have that be your guide. Avoid getting distracted by side projects. Take your time and be realistic. Doing so will ensure that you follow through.

Then, Hunt and Gather

Find inspiration in images from magazines, book jackets, a print from a favorite skirt, the color of Italian gelato. Let go of all the rules! Pull in anything that speaks to you and your sense of place. Gather sparks and tidbits, not exact blueprints to copy. Compile them in a folder or create a large pin board in your home that you can walk by, add to, remove from, and change as you like.

Now take a breath and enjoy. Let's make your house a home.

CREATE YOUR FLOW

Pay attention to how you move from room to room and within a room to establish a flow that you enjoy. The more you can create purpose in your space, the closer you will get to its fullest potential.

When you hear the word *flow,* what comes to mind? It could be an easy movement, a series of yoga postures, how your eye tracks color in a painting, or how you move seamlessly from one room to another. Flow transcends culture and all forms of styling—you might have heard of *feng shui,* an ancient Chinese system of creating harmony in a space, including a home. Imagine how air circulates to keep an environment warm or cool: You want to avoid having any blockage—the aim is for a natural current. That's a flow. I know the flow is working at home when the whole space makes sense, there's a natural movement, and I feel welcomed every time I enter the front door. The flow is how my home puts me at ease; if it's missing, I become agitated.

Flow is an essential element. All day long, we move through all sorts of spaces—some are noisy and chaotic, others are quiet and calm. Some may produce stress or be relaxing and serene. After a typical nonstop day at the office, on set at a photo shoot for a new product, or running around to appointments and events, the flow of my home becomes super important.

Considering flow as a fundamental principle both for individual rooms and for all rooms combined can be a touchstone for thinking about your space, and for making your home more reflective of who you are and how you feel.

How Does the Layout Make a House a Home?

I moved my bed recently. This change may seem small, but it had a major impact. I'd assumed the bed should be placed where it could have maximum space around it. The head was against the wall to my right when I walked in the bedroom, so when I entered my room, I was walking into the side of the bed. Only small nightstands would fit beside it, and the aesthetics were off balance. The room lacked perspective and warmth.

Now the head of the bed is on the wall opposite the door. It extends into the middle of the room, becoming the clear focal point when you enter. Suddenly, the room's purpose is clear. Why have all that empty space in the room? I wasn't entertaining guests there. This is where I wake up from a restful sleep and it becomes my retreat at the end of the day. Of course the bed is the centerpiece! I gave up the empty space that had been at the foot of the bed for a more balanced, purposeful layout, adding more functional and pleasing nightstands plus a proper headboard. Entering my bedroom, I am now met by a flow that invites me to rest, sleep, and rejuvenate.

What seemed a simple act transformed my most personal space into one that provided what I truly needed. To achieve this essential sense of flow, I considered how the function of the space intersected with the fit of all the separate pieces. The function of my bedroom—sleeping and retreating—was more fully realized by adjusting the furniture, so each component better contributed to the whole.

Look at each room in your home and identify the visual cue when you walk in. If your living room is all about lounging and getting cozy, you might make a plush sectional your centerpiece. If you collect art books, an oversized coffee table or one with two tiers provides ample space to display them. Counter stools in the kitchen invite people to gather and participate. This concept carries through to your whole house, too: Form and function come together when you identify the way each room and area can be both visually appealing and useful.

When recalling that simply moving my bed achieved the focal point and visual harmony I was seeking, I recognized this to be achieving the flow. The point of attention became clear. Flow is less about conventional floor plans (two chairs, a coffee table, and a sofa) and more about discovering a room's intention. How do you cultivate a sense of well-being and flow in your home? By identifying the purpose, a natural layout will present itself.

If there is an overarching story for a home, there's also a narrative for each room.

These are the questions to ask yourself to define your room's purpose:

What am I working with?
Start with the realities of your home. Note the highlights, such as a working fireplace, and the challenges, like an odd-shaped nook. From there, you can quickly and clearly assess the layout plan that puts your home's best features on display while minimizing any flaws.

What's most important to me?
I like entertaining, so that drives many of my choices in the living room, dining room, kitchen, and outdoors. If your home doubles as an office, you may want multiple spaces where you can land with your laptop to spread out for a project. With children, open play areas seem to take over. These key influencers set your priorities.

What's the purpose here?
Walk from room to room and imagine yourself using the space optimally. Ask, "What do I do here? What would make it better?" If you love to practice yoga and meditate, create an attractive corner with your

yoga mat and candles. If you are an avid reader or writer or painter, let your interest or craft be integral to your design.

TIP Keep room measurements stored in your phone. I stumbled upon a great dresser when out to brunch with friends and having these on hand made my purchase decision easy.

Acknowledge the Architecture

My approach is to embrace what you have, use it, and maximize its possibilities. The architectural frame can help you articulate and emphasize your home's story, or you can play with contrast, filling a room with surprising design. While curved archways and built-ins convey a more relaxed, lived-in look and crown molding and high ceilings read as more formal, that doesn't mean these details have to dictate how you live. In fact, carrying out a specific architectural style down to every piece of furniture and accent will make it feel more like a museum or dollhouse than a personal interior.

A bungalow can never be an industrial loft. But creative contrast adds intrigue to the design—think of a low-slung modern sofa in a classical brownstone or an English credenza along a white plaster wall in a Spanish Colonial. The magic lies in the mix. So acknowledge your house's framework, and also envision how you want to live within it.

Identify the Anchors

Every room needs a central focal point, a place to start, then build around. Usually, it's a sofa in a living room, a table in a dining space, or a bed in a bedroom. But remember: You can and should forgo conventions if they don't work for you. If your entertaining style is more casual and bohemian and you have a low table that you love, make an intimate conversation circle with layered rugs and lots of floor pillows. You might have furniture you can easily move when guests visit or when you have game night and shift the focus altogether. If you work at home, you might prioritize a space for creative thinking. Your anchor may be an inspired desk appointed with essentials to ensure you want to spend time there each day.

Create Visual Language

The way you arrange furniture suggests what to do in a room. The two matching chairs in my living room are telling people to go over there and sit and talk—they say conversation corner. Pick any room in your house. Stand in the spot where you can achieve the broadest perspective. What's the story you see? Is this the story you want to tell, or is there another that compels you more?

Each room is a chapter in a book that becomes your home's story. The rooms can have different intentions and feels. In fact, I think they should. Ultimately, how they all connect and combine makes the flow of the home.

Once you have acknowledged and thought about the existing architecture, room anchors, and visual story, consider these simple guidelines that can help you achieve a floor plan that looks and feels like you.

Scale and Proportion Matter

When I think of scale and proportion, I consider how the furniture or art pieces fit in the particular room, how they relate to one another, and how I feel in the space. In a small seating area, an oversized couch that fills it up can be inviting. If you want a room to appear larger and airier, think about opting for pieces that have slim profiles and lighter fabrics, or use glass or acrylic pieces that allow light to pass through. Think about the horizontal lines—what you see at eye level—and then also the vertical lines—how you are using the height of the room. You can accentuate a high ceiling with a tall floor lamp or large tree. A lower ceiling could have dark paint with adjacent white walls for an intimate or moody statement. A room has many dimensions. Your home is like a puzzle; the joy comes from reimagining, rearranging, and exploring options.

If there is an overarching story for a home, there's also a narrative for each room.

Determining Function

Flow in key areas means that you can move easily, what you need is within reach, and the purpose is clear. When considering movement and function, I divide my home into retreat spaces, passing spaces, and entertaining spaces.

Retreat Spaces: Bedroom, Bath, Office

These spots are the most personal. They're where you go to escape the world, unwind, refresh, or get something accomplished. If these areas feel weighed down by too much furniture or limited space to move in and out or around the desk, chair, or bed, then they won't work. When the flow is working, the room is inviting; you want to be in the space and it's easy to be there.

You spend considerable time in your retreats, so make comfort a priority. Think about what you need when you wake up, and what you want at the end of a long day—and if it's relevant, in between. Is it cocoon-like, or does it have a clean, bright, minimalist vibe? Imagine a physical manifestation of a deep, cleansing sigh. What do you see around you? If it is a space just for you, there are no limitations. If you're sharing the space with someone, combine both of your favorites to make it work.

For a clarifying view, stand in the middle of each room, including your bathroom. Take a 360-degree look and see what is appealing and what is most magnetic. What pulls you in, and what raises questions like, "Why is this here?" For flow, I always think less is more. And in these retreat rooms, flow is most important.

Passing Spaces: Entry, Hallway, Stairs, Spaces Between Furniture

Which spaces (or areas within a space) contribute to or inhibit an easy flow within the home? Does the design make moving easy or is there a misplaced chair or unfortunate clutter? A passing space may be small—just between furniture—or more significant, like an entryway or hallway.

Let's start at the beginning. Leave. Seriously. Walk out the front door, pause, and walk back in. What catches your eye? Where do you most naturally want to move? What color is most noticeable? Is any feeling aroused? We all know about first impressions: they matter. What does coming home really feel like—and what is the first impression guests have when they arrive?

Think about what you want to see when you walk in each day. For me, it's order and calm. And I appreciate a pop of inspiration. You may be surprised to find how quickly you're able to assess what to adjust or add, be it a splash of wallpaper, a big mirror, or a chair.

In passing spaces, one of two things tend to happen: They either become a depot for anything we don't want to put in our other rooms, or they are ignored and become bare and cold, feeling disconnected from other spaces. Both are missed opportunities that disrupt the flow. In our bodies, it's the connective tissue that we rely on to move, run, and sit. In a home, these connectors are either subtle or significant transitions. Either way they are part of the story.

Halls and stairways are often neglected because we move through them; we don't linger. But they still matter. They offer another opportunity to evoke feeling and express yourself.

Do these spaces have ample light that can add warmth? You may be able to add a bit of function with a narrow chest or dresser that can hold linens or games or photo albums. Think about style possibilities. Could this be a perfect place for a gallery arrangement of artwork or photography? Since these are spaces you move through, you can have a bit of fun with bold wallpaper or a vibrant paint color. Or take a

minimalist approach—my friend left her curved staircase purposefully void of art for a calming feeling that works because it contrasts with her art-filled home.

Passing space exists within each room as well, mostly between furniture but also at each individual entry point. If the purpose of the room has been solidly defined and designed, that will come across immediately. Imagine what the movement will be like inside—or literally take a spin through it. Double-check for safety that there is nothing to trip or stumble over. Be sure there's ample room to get around the corner chair so you aren't bumping into a side table. My living room furniture is close together, but the flow around this cluster makes it easy to get up and greet people as they enter or head into the kitchen. You want your rooms to serve many purposes—but not at the expense of overall comfort. Aim for functionality and flexibility.

You want your rooms to serve many purposes—but not at the expense of overall comfort. Aim for functionality and flexibility.

Entertaining Spaces: Living Room, Dining Room, Kitchen, Patio, Balcony, Backyard

Places where you welcome people should look and feel instantly open and inviting, and not overly formal—unless that's your style. The flow in such areas will help you entertain with ease, and should work equally well when you are alone or with just a friend or two.

I aim for seating that is comfortable for me and flexible for gatherings. I like to have options that work whether my friends and I are hanging out watching movies or having a casual brunch. There are practical considerations to keep in mind: Are there enough surfaces where guests can eat or put down their drinks? Enough pillows for quick seating options? Consider if some of the chairs, stools, or benches in other rooms can do double duty for a spontaneous gathering. I keep a basket of throws in my living room, so they are ready to grab for outside evening events if it's a little chilly.

People need to have choices for sitting and standing and moving around. My friends typically gather around food. I aim to guide the flow by strategically placing the guacamole and chips in one area and more substantial fare on the patio near the grill. The combination of wine and water on the dining room table and an open cooler with a variety of drinks outside keeps people moving.

The dining room deserves a cautionary warning. It can easily become cluttered and tight depending on the size of your table and chairs, and whether you have a sideboard, credenza or cabinets, a bar cart, rug, and heavy drapes. I aim for an intimate space where less is more. I want to be able to pull away the chairs and have people move around the table easily. Stand where you can get a view of the dining area and observe whether it's easy to navigate, or needs a bit of pruning.

A kitchen serves a myriad of purposes and is often a gathering hub. Whether you're prepping salad for an intimate lunch or making chili for a party, the nonstop activity and aromas are an automatic draw. If you have an open floor plan, consider adding counter stools to draw people in.

Each space outside requires two sets of eyes: one for me when I'm alone and another for friends. My patio has two lounge chairs, an L-shaped sofa, and a picnic-style table and umbrella where I can relax with a book, have a conversation, set up an impromptu call with my office, or put out a brunch spread. The layout affords me options—and that's part of an effective flow. Even during a cold winter, a balcony can be a draw for hearty folks during parties, with table and chairs year-round.

Lighting and music both set the tone and mood and contribute to the flow of my home. A cluster of candles gathers my friends in the living room and whatever music we play sets the vibe. (See more on pages 73 and 179.)

Balance Is Key

I am often looking at how things fit together. If I walk into a room and something is off, and it continues to bother me, that's a sign of imbalance. When I have this sense, I aim to identify a root cause. Are the shapes off? For example, a round coffee table in front of a long sectional couch may not work because it's out of proportion with the seating and doesn't extend far enough for easy use. Does the leather side chair seem to be isolated from the other pieces of furniture because it needs a companion chair to give it purpose?

While mixing shapes and styles can be great, they still have to blend together for a cohesive feel. We are looking for the Swedish concept of *lagom*—just the right amount. You can achieve lagom by following Goldilocks's lead: Too much? Too little? Or just right? I love how lagom reminds us to slow down and find what is relaxing and satisfying. These practical cues guide us to balance. We seek a similar balance with a great meal. My default is to aim for a bit less, whether taking a serving of dessert or wondering if I can squeeze one more chair into a sitting area. Less helps me strike that perfect balance.

2

SHOW YOUR TRUE COLORS

Color is design shorthand. Tones and shades instantly set a mood, express a feeling, and create a sensation within your home. Take time to find the hues that speak to you.

Color—or lack of color—is probably the first thing you will notice in a space. Color is where your story begins. Consider how you feel in different spaces. Have you ever surprised yourself by falling in love with a monochromatic room? And then five minutes later stepped into a space overflowing with color splashes and felt pure delight? These experiences reinforce this idea that color is an external expression of all the emotions we feel—from serious to playful and everything in between.

Like any other design choice, it's not about what's *right* or what is trending. It's about what palette you want to live with. How does color make you feel, and how do you want people to feel when they come over?

When I come home, I want colors that are easy on the eye. My home offers a mix of expressions through varied hues and shades. There is warmth in the background and pops of color that energize and add elements of surprise. I can play with color by adding a bouquet of protea, a small flatweave rug, or a framed vintage oil painting. Color is how I explore my aesthetic and express creativity.

Since colors are also what I depend upon for feeling refreshed and revitalized at every time of day, I aim for variety. A kitchen backsplash can add a cup of cheerful to a recipe. Linen bedding in a bone or blush color in my bedroom creates a dreamy tone to relax and restore. Color is always how I accent and enhance my space, set a vibe, and build a story. What I particularly love are the endless options and diverse possibilities.

Look out the window. Nature offers endless clues for combinations that are both soothing, unexpected, and filled with life. Color inspiration is everywhere! In a restaurant, when a chef is plating, she is considering how food is more than taste—it's also about composition of color and texture. An illustrator of a children's book makes choices for visual intrigue and to create a bit of awe on each page. Find the color wherever you go!

Color *is* the story. If you're seeking to turn your space into a sanctuary that emanates calm and relaxation, or that boosts creativity and vitality, the solution may be just a few paint strokes away.

How Does Color Make a House a Home?

We experience the link between color and mood all the time. We naturally gravitate toward colors that help us feel more peaceful or energetic or stimulate a memory. Because of its association with nature, I find green to be a particularly soothing color. A soft yellow brings up fond memories of my childhood bedroom. Color is personal. Keep in mind that selecting colors based on the choices other people are making is not the best way to find your true colors.

My perspective on color has evolved over time. I have been influenced by being in different cities, particularly New York and now Los Angeles, and by living in different spaces with and without others.

New York was the first place I lived alone, so I actively experimented to find my sense of style there. I incorporated color to counteract the surrounding "concrete jungle," and of course, not everything worked. Knowing what *didn't* work became as important as noticing what did. It was through this experimentation that I thrived, and found an inherent sense of play. When you walked into my apartment you would see a white wall; I added a large orange decal of a grandfather clock. One day I impulsively color-coordinated my bookshelf, thereby shifting the focus when you entered the living room. And when I outgrew the orange clock and colored book arrangement, I tried something new.

When I moved back to L.A., where I was born and raised, I revisited my roots with a fresh perspective. I found new appreciation for and inspiration in the Southern California landscape: the bright morning sky with towering palm trees; the sunset and the soft dusk on the coast. I am equal parts beach and desert, both of which influence the neutral palette that has become my signature. Some people prefer bright, bold colors everywhere. I admire that aesthetic, but I find an innate comfort and calm in the neutral zone. It's where I feel most confident and grounded. I didn't come to this realization overnight; it was by being repeatedly drawn to these tones that I discovered what is most authentically me. But I enjoy exceptions to any rule: If I'm captivated by a red dress or a bright, colorful abstract art piece, that's another part of my expression.

It's important to distinguish between colors you admire and those you want to surround yourself with. I was once mesmerized by a hotel lobby outfitted with jewel tones, colorful tile, and ornate details; but I know it's not what I want to live with every day. My muted palette allows me to introduce bits of color to a space without losing the overall tone. I have never been a blue person, but I fell in love with a cobalt blue lamp. With no other blue in the room where I placed it, the lamp offered a bite of freshness and surprise. Every time I see it, I pause with satisfaction and delight. This, too, is me.

To find your home's palette, think about some basic truths around your natural color leanings, as well as the feelings you want to create room to room. There are no absolutes when it comes to color.

What colors am I most drawn to?

I recommend looking in two places to answer this question. First, take a peek in your closet. If your clothing is mostly blue, gray, and tan, you might gravitate toward similar colors or tones at home. If you see a lot of bold color, you may lean toward a dark paint or deep shade of upholstery. Then, look at the photo roll in your camera or phone. Do you tend to take more pictures of sunsets, greenery, and muted shades, or bolder hues? These may provide hints to what your eye is most drawn to.

What's the mood I want?

When it comes to your home's overall story, color is a huge indicator of mood. Think about the feeling you want to create. Different spaces

may lead you to different answers—typically calm in the bed or bath, cheerful in the kitchen, and cozy and intimate in the living room. When you identify the energy you want to generate, think about your personal color associations. For me, calm is neutrals, soft grays, and pale blues. Cheerful brings out the yellow and rose hues. A more intimate setting would blend neutrals with some darker overtones, especially greens and burgundy. Your palette should incorporate colors of varying moods so you can achieve the ambience you want.

How will the room be used?

Color accentuates how light is reflected. It influences a brighter or darker setting. An office space benefits from inspiring colors and a warm, clean appearance, which can help keep you awake and focused. With a baby's room, you'll want to avoid colors that are too bright or agitating; it's best to use calming, subtle colors with a nurturing vibe. In a living room, I find my widest set of color options since it's the most versatile in how the space is used. If you want to be adventurous with colors, this is the place to do it. Considering how a room is used will help you narrow or broaden your choices while still having options within each color scheme.

When these same colors, or similar shades or hues, connect from room to room, you contribute to the visual flow.

Find Your Palette

A palette is basically your color themes; you can find yours even if you skipped Art 101. I start by discovering the shade of white that may appear on a wall, the ceiling, or a door and window trim. White is necessary in your palette because it combines with everything. After that, choose three to five colors for your base to provide variety without being too chaotic. With your white and your base set, you can adjust your tones, make subtle adaptations, introduce a new color altogether, or decide to skip one color for a specific room. If you have a defining color element in the room that is not changing, like a dark wood floor or a single forest-green wall, that becomes part of your base palette by default. Be sure the other colors complement rather than clash. When these same colors, or similar shades or hues, connect from room to room, you contribute to the visual flow.

Universally Flattering Palettes

There are a few combinations that, unsurprisingly, mimic nature, and work in any room, any design, any location. They are classic without feeling dated, modern without leaving the room (or you) feeling cold.

Sunset Hues: sand, dusty rose, faded yellow, muted coral
New Neutrals: charcoal, white, cream, silver, black
Shades of Blue: indigo, deep blue, chambray, cloud
Modern Earthy: oatmeal, clay, ocher, chocolate brown, terra-cotta

Mixing It Up

Can you take a warm and fiery color and combine it with a romantic and alluring color? Of course. That's how a palette becomes unique and personal. Deep orange and plum may work together when balanced

Color Stories

Cool & Calming
The colors: sea blue, cream, white, pale green, gray, beige, mauve
What they convey: tranquility, lightness, order, quiet
Where they may work: bedroom, bath, office, kitchen, nursery

Warm & Fiery
The colors: poppy red, deep orange, bright yellow
What they convey: energy, spirit, warmth, happiness
Where they may work: kitchen, dining room, family room

Romantic & Alluring
The colors: lavender, deep pink, plum, dark brown, jade green
What they convey: luxury, nostalgia, femininity, mystery
Where they may work: entry, bedroom, living room

Clean & Distinct
The colors: black, white, cream, gray
What they convey: artful restraint, classicism, elegance
Where they may work: kitchen, bath, office, bedroom, living room,
dining room

with a crisp bright white that lets the natural light bounce off and brighten the space. Your foundational palette for your home keeps the look cohesive. Individual rooms can be treated separately, with additional colors or tones enhancing the space as you like.

TIP Does It Pass the Test? No matter what hue you select, test it first. Ask for a tester can of your selected paint or a swatch of wallpaper and cover at least a two-by-four foot patch of wall. Is it appealing at different times of the day as the light changes? Do you still love it after a week? If the answers are yes, it's the right one for you. If not, keep looking.

Saying It with Color and Pattern

Paint and wallpaper are easy, intriguing ways to make a statement—bold or subtle—with a can and brush or roll and paste. These tools allow your style and personality to shine. How will you choose to make your home expressive and inviting?

Paint

Painting a **bright or deep color** on just one wall brightens a room by creating contrast against the other white or lighter color walls. Contrast creates intentional opposition and interest that can add depth or intrigue.

Make your own art by painting **abstract lines, stripes, or swooping curves** on your walls or ceilings. Use painter's tape or the appropriate stencil for a finished look. This one-of-a-kind expression can draw the eye, become a conversation starter, or visually alter the room's dimensions.

Use **color blocking** for an instant architectural splash. This popular approach takes a cue from contemporary fashion styles. On a single-color wall, select two different colors and use a geometric or angular pattern to establish calm (with modest contrast) or drama (with high contrast). Complementary tonal hues create a subtle, unique pattern, while bold contrasting colors direct the eye to a specific focal point.

Use paint with a **specialty finish** like a faux suede, metallic, or pebbled look to give depth and texture to a space. This is a striking way to add an edge or softness or to replicate the appearance of another material like concrete or a fabric.

Paint walls, ceiling, and trim **all the same hue.** It will create a seamless experience, making the walls recede and almost float away and giving more attention to the objects and furniture. If that's what's most important to you in the space, go for it!

Wallpaper

Wallpaper is an instant visual pop and runs the style gamut from subtle to fantastical. When I added a wallpaper accent wall in my baby's nursery, I did extensive shopping to find one that captured a playful feeling in my desired color tones. I settled on a whimsical pattern of palm trees and little tropical fruits—watermelon, pineapple, papaya. It added both depth and an eye-catching statement while still looking great with the room's wood and natural hues.

Use wallpaper to **define a space.** Open floor plans and big spaces can be separated into sections with wallpaper. For example, using wallpaper in a corner of your kitchen can instantly create a breakfast nook when complemented by a small table and chairs. You can slice it and dice it however you choose: Wallpaper just one wall or do three.

Use a light-colored wallpaper with thin horizontal lines to **make a room feel larger.** A dark, large-scale pattern will **envelop a space to make it cozier.**

Create a **jewel-box moment** by papering a small powder room, closet, the back of shelving, or the bottom of drawers.

If a room looks too monochromatic or you want to add flair, **cover a pair of lampshades** with wallpaper or use some **under a glass-topped table.**

Wallpaper the **ceiling** for an unexpected pop of pattern—anything from dots to stripes to a beautiful floral design. Doing so can add warmth, height, or intimacy to a room.

Use wallpaper as an **accessory.** It can be used to create a simple, space-saving headboard in the bedroom, or a kitchen backsplash in lieu of tile.

Connect with Color

Color isn't only for your walls; it's also for the drapes, rugs, cushions, throws, and art. In fact, color is everywhere. Conscious coloring means your home reflects your ideas, preferences, and sense of expression. There are plenty of ways to add hues to your home. Try these light-touch, instant color ideas.

Wall-to-wall carpets add color that is literally an understatement since they are not at eye level. By covering a larger area, the impact of color and texture is somewhat diffused. Whether lighter or darker, carpet makes a statement, so ensure any wall-to-wall carpets set a foundation you will enjoy. If it's something you inherited in the space and it's not your ideal choice, work with it until you can switch it out, or consider layering a rug on top of it.

Area rugs offer a quick intro to color and pattern and they work with all kinds of flooring, even on top of wall-to-wall carpet. They can unify and define a conversation corner or a dining area set up in an open space. From the bathroom to the kitchen to the bedroom, area rugs in these spaces give an immediate color and texture boost.

Swapping out a white **lampshade** for a colorful one is a low-risk, high-reward move. Solids, patterns, florals, and pleats each add a different color motif. They can cast a moodier light in the room if you are looking for instant atmosphere. Feel like doing it yourself? Fabric dye or spray paint can update a lampshade with a personal touch. Or try tea staining to create an antique look.

Curtain panels or window shades add color in small, structured doses. It's your choice: A color that blends into the wall makes these additions nearly invisible, or you can make them pop with color contrast. Make one choice per room—but feel free to vary your expression from room to room.

Framed artwork and photographs deliver doses of color while also adding depth and texture. Your options are limitless. If you have room to store a few extra pieces, you can easily make changes when you're ready for something new and fresh. These swaps can perk up a room with minimal effort. My living room wall is a constant work in process as I switch out bright abstract pieces for a big landscape photograph just because.

Have fun with **accessories.** These accents are your signature, and often are a collection of memories. If, like me, you lean toward a neutral palette, a yellow glass bowl placed in a foyer to hold mail and keys adds brightness. A cluster of different-sized colored vases on a bar cart may contribute to an energizing mood. Enjoy the mobility of these items and change them out or relocate them occasionally.

Smaller **upholstered pieces** like a footstool, pouf, or side chair can introduce a little color while serving a purpose. Go for contrast with such pieces that can move from place to place.

Pillows are an easy color fix. With options in all shapes and sizes, you can combine color and comfort. Pick one color or a mix to add flair to your cream-colored couch. Or if your couch is bolder, use neutral pillows to mellow it out.

3

LET THERE BE LIGHT

Every room is touched and transformed by light, both its presence and its absence. Play with natural and artificial lighting to lift your spirits, heighten energy for productivity, or create a soothing ambience.

Lighting influences how you experience each and every part of your home. But it is often considered at the end of the decorating process, well after layout and furniture finishes—and that's late in the game. Lighting is an essential ingredient and will always be present, so figure out how to make it work for you. Think about and prioritize its effect on how rooms look and how you feel in them.

I grew up in L.A. where natural light is idyllic for much of the year. Living on the East Coast for nearly thirteen years, I learned how to accentuate natural light as the seasons changed—making adaptations even with cloudy or snowy skies. During my first New York winter, I recognized how important light is to the feeling of home. It can warm a space to counteract an extended inclement season, or it can enhance the cozy rainy-day feeling if that's your preference. I knew I wanted to bring that Southern California light into my cramped apartment. A challenge, I'll admit, but through trial and error, it became clear that just one type of light or light source does not solve everything.

In New York, the natural light from one medium-sized window in my bedroom was insufficient. The permanent overhead light was a start. I added smaller lamps on the bedside tables and one on my desk. But something was still missing. I made a significant purchase of an extremely tall floor lamp with a pivoting shade and adjustable body. I was looking for a striking piece to accent my large room and it served both purposes. From its position in the corner, the lamp could be extended for lighting in different vignettes, servicing my desk, couch area, and bed.

I want each room to have flexibility when it comes to light. Realizing I could use multiple sources rather than be bound by just the overhead light was a game changer. After work, when I'm in relax mode, I want dimness throughout the house. It's a deep contrast to the blast of light I crave and achieve by opening all the blinds first thing in the morning. I have worked to maximize the fixed and flexible lighting elements in each room.

How Does Light Make a House a Home?

Optimal lighting is both uplifting and calming. Light induces productivity when needed and can be adapted to produce a cheerful mood when work is done. With lighting you can make quick adjustments; however, you have to plan ahead and think through possibilities. Doing so means diversifying lighting sources, having ample options available, and clarifying your priorities. What do you need to wake up, refresh yourself, read a magazine, settle down at the end of the day, or create a memorable moment for guests? These considerations will affect how you select your fixtures, sources, and even your dimmers.

Finding your optimal lighting scheme is key. Spend time in each space. Sit. Read. Watch TV. Host guests. Run through all the actions of your routine. Answer these questions to put together a lighting design that works for you:

What light do I crave?
You might love soft moodiness, or maybe you prefer crisp brightness. Or you might want both in the same day. Do you crave warm, bright, inviting, soft, smooth, restful, active, cool, celebratory, or romantic lighting? For an upbeat, joyful mood, light reflecting off of objects creates a sparkling effect. For a more intimate moment, select lower levels of light to flatter the faces and draw attention inward. Being able to make quick adjustments is one reason I have dimmers everywhere. My home has to readily transform with my desires.

What's already here?

Assess what is installed in your home—chandeliers, pendants, sconces, and so on. Decide what you like as is, or what needs to be updated. As you clarify the primary purpose of each room, you can determine what alterations or additions are needed. Aim for quality of light rather than sheer quantity.

How does the light change?

Natural light changes all day, so determine which crevice or corner may need a boost in the evening. Incorporating varied light sources can give you maximum usage all day long.

Maximizing Natural Light

Sunshine brings me joy when I'm outside, so I bring it inside wherever I can. My preference is to wake up early and start to wind down when the sun is setting. Following the natural light cues of the day is my ideal, though it's not always possible. I constantly consider ways I can enhance what natural light I have in each space.

Dress windows lightly
Dark fabrics absorb light. Translucent shades and panels take sunlight further and add a breezy, easy feeling. I default to lighter fabrics for my bedroom window treatments, even if it means I wake up earlier. If privacy is an issue, use gauzy layers.

Use transparent doors and screens
Switch out one or more of your exterior and interior wooden doors for one with glass panels. If you're concerned about security, add frosted film, which provides privacy but still lets light through. Having a screen on my back door lets me keep it open for the breeze and light.

Clean your windows
Keeping the panes dirt- and dust-free allows light to stream in.

Choose glassy furniture
Glass-top and acrylic tables let natural light move throughout a room.

Layering Light

A mix of light sources adds texture and tone, creates highlights and lowlights, and establishes functional contrast. While you can't switch out your sofa on a whim, you can turn off an overhead light, turn on a lamp, and add a few candles to make a significant difference. To enliven, illuminate, and create versatile lighting, think about combining these sources:

Ambient lighting
I think of ambient lighting as the soft background music of the room. This is your base and it is always present. It's a combination of the natural lighting from your windows and the most general artificial lighting, like an overhead. Ambient light establishes everyday comfort without glare. You can add to and alter ambient lighting with any type of fixture.

Accent lighting
Lamps, sconces, and pendants highlight specific areas or vignettes such as artwork, a dining area, or a nightstand. Floor and table lamps add to a space beyond just the light they cast; they can be statement pieces, adding sculptural zing and providing pops of color and texture— an additional way to accessorize.

Task lighting
Directed bright light meets the need of a specific purpose like reading, prepping in the kitchen, or applying makeup. The most practical of our light sources, a task light can be altered with bulbs, finish, and shapes. Lamps can also have dimmers so that even a task lamp by day can contribute to a different mood by night.

Lighting sets your tone. Your choices literally illuminate the functional and aesthetic elements of your home.

Unscented candles

While scented candles can be ideal in small doses for a particular mood or setting, skipping the scent brings the focus onto the flickering light, the ambience, and the shadows created. A cluster of candles in front of a fireplace or a single candle on a mantel draws the eye and adds warmth. Candles can be placed atop a table runner in the dining room while the overhead light stays dim.

TIP Want to instantly change a room from bright work light to moody, chill light? Repeat after me: dimmer. They also save energy and are easy for an electrician to install.

The Right Light

Planning a lighting scheme ahead of time will help you avoid costly mistakes. Walk through your home to map out the specific type of light you want in each space. If you love to cook, you'll want bright light in the kitchen for chopping garlic and reading recipes. If your bedroom is meant to be serene and soothing, you will likely seek the opposite. Lighting sets your tone. Your choices literally illuminate the functional and aesthetic elements of your home.

You want a **bedroom** to feel light, bright, and lively in the morning and cozy and relaxing when you turn in. A good-sized overhead fixture adds a bit of drama and casts soft light after the sun goes down. For reading in bed, choose swing-arm sconces or table lamps tall enough to put a spotlight on your book. Optimize your natural light with pale curtains and shades. If you don't like the morning light to rouse you, include blackout shades for sleeping in.

The **bath** needs honest yet flattering light for putting on makeup and general primping. Install versatile window treatments that allow for privacy, and can be opened easily to let in natural light. Overhead light alone, most common in bathrooms, creates shadows and often casts harsh shadows. Add a pair of sconces that flank the mirror. Hanging them at eye level will bring light in that sweeps across your face. A bathroom really calls out for a dimmer and a stash of candles for relaxing tub time.

A **living room** generally needs flexible window treatments and lighting as the room's function changes from hour to hour and from one day to the next. You might be doing work there on a weekday and hosting casual cocktails come Saturday night. Choose a number of task and floor lamps instead of just one overhead light. For added interest, mix up lamp shapes and shades. Add three-way bulbs for different moods. Pretty candlesticks of varying heights create extra ambience.

As an entertaining space, the **dining room** calls for warm light. Choose window treatments that allow for natural light but can easily be drawn to set a darker, moody tone. A chandelier or other notable fixture is common above a dining table because it adds dimension through its height and drama through its design. You gain both adaptable light (assuming you have a dimmer) and a statement piece to congregate under, sort of like gathering around a campfire. Be sure the scale is right and the light is suitable for dinner for two as well as for a larger group. A table lamp or a pair of sconces warms up a sideboard or buffet.

If a **kitchen** lacks windows to provide ample natural light, your fixture choices will really matter. Here, the duality of purpose is key. There is the functional aspect that requires a brighter light—typically overhead lighting for overall illumination when chopping, dicing, peeling, and grating for meal preparation. But the kitchen is also used as a gathering hub for conversation and wine when friends arrive or for a weeknight countertop dinner. Diverse lighting and dimmers once again let you adjust and adapt for all the ways you enjoy your kitchen.

Provide a warm welcome in the **entry or hall.** Pay attention to any natural lighting at different times of day to determine what will work best with overhead lighting, sconces, or a table lamp. A row of pendants adds an artistic flair.

Do your **closets** have the appropriate lighting to help you find that lost slipper or grab the correct navy blazer? Some closet lights turn on automatically when you open the doors. Others are standard fare with a switch or cord. Be sure you get the appropriate wattage so the colors shine true and you can keep items organized and accessible.

Before

TIP With all the lamps and fixtures, you also have cords. There are do-it-yourself solutions—like using foam core board as a faux wall under a desk to hide any cords. Or you can find an inexpensive cord organizer wherever you purchase home supplies; these help reduce clutter and visibility. Even more affordable—and easy: Use tape and adhesive sticky hooks to secure cords to the backs of tables or sofas. If you have the option, run cords behind the walls.

After

Lighten Up

A bright feel to a room is a mood enhancer. If your space lacks natural light, consider incorporating the below remedies over time. You might already have some of them working in your favor or they may be possible if you make easy adjustments. Others will be a bonus as you continue curating your home.

Paint walls a light color

Your palette can make or break the mood. The lighter your large surfaces, the more reflective light you'll get. As light reflects, or bounces off a surface, more of it is visible—and light changes the way objects look. For maximum reflective light, a white ceiling adds a lift and a white gloss brings shine to baseboards and doors. Select lighter shades of blues, yellows, greens. Satin finish reflects light more than a matte finish.

Hang a mirror

Light loves a reflective surface. A mirror directly across from a large window can double the sunlight. The frame can turn the mirror into an artistic statement as well. Even mirrored accessories accentuate the light. Proper placement enlarges the room overall.

Add more lamps

Bring 'em on. If the natural light is spare, shine artificial light to augment whatever is available. If you are running out of tabletop space or have maxed out on floor lamps, consider a wall-mounted option (one of my personal favorites).

Bright Ideas

People, including me, are often flustered by the available array of bulbs. Here are the basics:

Incandescents
Slowly fading away in favor of energy-efficient bulbs, these classic models produce a glowing light that is ultraflattering and adds a warm feeling.

Compact Fluorescent Bulbs (CFLs)
Using 75 percent less energy than incandescents, these bulbs emit a cooler tone and come in a wide range of brightness.

LEDs
Energy efficient and very long-lasting, these are often used for task lighting and have a cooler, harsher light. Many cast a light similar to that of incandescents.

Halogens
Halogens cast a bright white light that feels like natural daylight, which makes them great for task lighting. They use a bit less energy than incandescent bulbs.

Aesthetic Bulbs
Edison bulbs with their vintage feel and silver bowls that are dipped in a metallic finish are both pretty enough to stand alone sans shade. Edison bulbs have an amber tone for a moody accent when the rest of the room is darker. Choose silver bowl bulbs to reduce offensive glare, ideal when you prefer an indirect source of light. These kinds of specialty bulbs are meant to be exposed and are best used when the fixture itself is more subtle.

Simulate the sky

If you have skylights, double down on keeping them clean. If you are considering them, know that they are a somewhat steep investment, but bring ample rewards. They promote light when you don't have traditional windows. Sun tunnels are an easier and more affordable solution in places where windows and skylights are not an option. There is no view or ventilation. Instead, light bounces off a sheet-metal tube to target light anywhere in the home, like a hallway, closet, or windowless room.

4

GET IN TOUCH

Textiles touch you—a rug under your feet, a throw pillow against your back, bedding you slip into each night. Find the fabrics that weave your home together, and that add distinct texture and depth to your individual rooms.

believe textiles are the most versatile and transformative elements in a home. We all have preferences for different physical sensations and these essential layers are all about personal comfort. Whether I am cuddling on my leather couch under an alpaca throw, being wrapped in a plush towel after a hot shower, or lingering between crisp cotton sheets and a linen duvet cover, I find the sensation to be desirable. We are tactile beings and textiles are both enjoyed in the moment and trigger memories of past experiences.

My love affair with textiles was sparked many years ago. While traveling in Italy, I checked into a picturesque hotel on the Amalfi Coast and discovered the softest, most sumptuous bedding. This experience awakened my curiosity about fabrics. Until then, textiles had just been a commodity I hadn't considered important. But after that, I began to notice that fabric influences comfort. I paid closer attention to the textiles all around me and the varied sensations they provoked. During my everyday morning and evening routines, I was enveloped in fabrics. With the right fabric choices, I was consistently more satisfied, whether drying dishes, showering, setting the table, fluffing a pillow, or sleeping. Textiles are a constant in my daily enjoyment of life.

This path took me on the unexpected journey to create Parachute, a home essentials brand born from this passion for comfort and wellness. We create products of the finest quality to help people start and end their days feeling their very best. We also pay close attention to how products are manufactured, eliminating toxic chemicals, artificial dyes, and synthetic finishes that impact our environment and personal health. I find joy in watching people interact with the textiles we create; it is an endless love story.

How Do Textiles Make a House a Home?

Textiles are everywhere in your home. Really, truly everywhere. They are your rugs, shower curtains, place mats, cushions, drapes, pillows, sheets, throws, and towels. I love the way textiles and textures change a room. The many varieties of fibers, weaving techniques, dyeing methods, and finishes make your rug, tablecloth, or bedspread what it is. Everything has a "handfeel"; that's your tactile experience of the fabric's texture, and how you perceive its warmth or coolness. The more you get your hands on different fabrics, the better you can determine what you like and what will enhance the comfort of your home. The textiles you choose—the ones you place on your bed and couch and floors and walls—add life to your rooms as you personalize each space.

What feel do I want?

I like having a variety of tactile options for the different experiences I crave in any given moment. The basket of throws in my den speaks to this notion: I can grab a light linen or a heavier alpaca at any time. You may already have preferences—a crisp, cool cotton in your bedsheets, for example. Experiment to find what feels good to you and when it feels good. With the vast assortment of textures available and places to implement them, your home can host a range of options that suit your personality and add to daily comfort. Switching out some of your textiles seasonally is an appealing option, too.

How do I balance form and function?

Style and use can combine to meet the various needs you have in your home. Remember that a fabric may look stunning, but it may not be suitable for how you really want to relax, play, entertain, or work.

Clarifying who will use the room—and how—can assist in determining your textiles. If you will have a steady stream of kids, live with a pet, or host a weekly meeting, you will benefit from a sturdy rug and a couch that's built to last and is easy to clean. If you eat at a kitchen counter most days, you can choose more delicate fabrics for dining room chair cushions.

What style am I seeking?

While you can combine varied styles in different rooms, an overarching preference will create a harmonious feel and should guide your fabric selections. If you gravitate toward:

Mid-Century Modern, you may like the clean, refined lines of cotton, linen, or wool

Industrial, you can underscore the exposed, minimalist look with leather, wool, and flatweave rugs

Bohemian, you'll be drawn toward the relaxed, easy feel of cotton blends, faux fur, velvet, and linen

Farmhouse, you can get rustic with linen, wool, cotton, and jute

Urban Modern, you can emphasize the sleek appeal with a fusion of cotton, cashmere, and silk

From your foundation, extend your reach to bring in additional textures. Make fabric and textiles your playground.

Light,
Airy

Warm,
Cozy

Textural,
Tonal

Textile Personalities

I tend to group fabrics by their characteristics and the feelings they bring into a house. My passion for fabrics makes me a constant learner—I enjoy introducing new textiles to influence the mood and flow of different areas. These three categories provide a primer for helping you find the feel for each part of your home.

Light, Airy

Linen: Linen is made from flax, producing the strongest fiber. This breathable fabric has a natural organic texture and continues to get softer with use. Great year-round, linen is a medium-weight fabric that keeps you cool in the summer and warm in the winter. Light, airy, and timeless, its casual elegance fits in any room.

Cotton: Versatile, breathable, and sturdy, cotton conveys a casual, laid-back message. Cottons are durable for homes with kids, dogs, and high-traffic areas. If you need a textile to be washable, it's the ideal choice. Cotton is woven into many favorite fabrics including percale, sateen, flannel, and twill.

Silk: A fabric with a luminous finish, silk instantly adds depth and glamour to a space. Because of its delicate nature, it's usually reserved for curtains and throw pillows rather than sofas or chairs.

Warm, Cozy

Velvet: Like silk, velvet conveys a more formal look and feel (think royalty), but it can be used casually depending on the silhouette—the shape or form—of a piece of furniture. Its smooth, shiny appearance is a strong texture statement and perfect for adding depth to a chair, sofa, or bench.

Wool: Natural and durable, wool is a favorite for pieces that experience wear and tear. It has a comforting texture that works well with cotton and linen pieces. Wool fabrics are wrinkle-resistant and have good elasticity, meaning they easily return to their original shape.

Leather: With its classic appeal, natural look, and graceful aging, leather gets warmer all the time. It can appear stately and fits well into a modern, casual look. Its durability is ideal for high-traffic areas, yet it is soft and comfortable.

Textured, Tonal

Suede: A leather fabric with a brushed finish, suede has a super soft, napped effect. It can feel relaxed or formal depending on what you pair it with. In little touches, it's a great fabric to add warmth and depth.

Jute: A super strong natural fiber, jute is rough to the touch; it feels organic and casual. Jute rugs are commonly used as a durable floor covering; they add a relaxed, coastal feel.

Hemp: An eco-friendly fabric like jute, hemp has an imperfect texture and can be hand-dyed in a rainbow of colors, or used to create block prints. It can stain easily, so keep that in mind when making choices. Hemp works well as a hallway or bedroom rug.

The Common Thread

If you look around most rooms, you will see how we use fabrics to soften hard edges, cover floors and windows, add accents, create contrast, and make our homes most livable.

If you are choosing **wall-to-wall-carpeting,** your focus is likely on maintenance, location for usage, the physical feel, and the scale of the pattern. Styles include a dense low-pile that works in high-traffic areas and higher-pile loop tips that are more cushiony and appropriate for lower-traffic spaces. Be sure to consult with experts to familiarize yourself with all the variables, including how the carpet is made, how to avoid any chemical residues, and whether natural fibers (like wool) will work or if synthetics are better.

Rugs are another major moment to bring on cozy feelings and tie a room together across living spaces. Once you have determined the size you need, think about your color and pattern. Consider the softness and the beauty you crave. You will find endless options of weaving techniques and fabrics. With hardwood floors, cotton and wool rugs create a soft landing for bare feet and can lend a splash of color or pattern. In my living room, I have a super plush rug with a cushiony feel. In the dining area, my handcrafted geometric flatweave kilim provides an attractive balance. Practicality and style played into both choices.

Window treatments add to the story of any room through the fabric you choose, and whether they are for privacy, to block light, or are purely decorative. Drapes soften an area filled with hard surfaces, and they can help a room feel extra soft and important when made of velvet, silk, or linen. Shades offer a more tailored look, and are better in spaces with smaller windows where drapes would look cluttered. Multiple layers are an option, too, for example, a wood shade covered by linen drapes. You can have the same system throughout the house or change it based on your priority room to room. Still, seek a compatible look so there's coherence and strong flow. Getting samples of any window treatment fabric lets you compare it against the paint color and fabrics on major pieces of furniture in the room.

Where you have room, a small **upholstered chair or fabric pouf** adds a layer of tactile punch and can be a clever place to stack towels (bathroom), books (living room), or games (den or kid's bedroom). Poufs and floor cushions are more than extra seating; they also bring texture and warmth. Leather, wool, and canvas versions work in most any space and for any style.

Similarly, think of **chair cushions** as an opportunity to add fun or vibrant fabric. It's a small hit that you can expose in a living room or tuck away in a dining room or office. Or, go for an **upholstered** look that adds a largely soft, unstructured piece while leather seats give you more structure and firmness. Cotton cushions can be subtle or striking. Depending on style, they can add comfort or be decorative—or both.

Decorative pillows in different fabrics and textures are easy ways to up the ante on style and comfort. Mix contrasting textiles to accent a couch, chair, or bed; try placing a modern linen square or lumbar shape on a canvas couch. A cozy alpaca pillow adds depth. Embroidered pillows, depending on their pattern, can range from subtle to bold. When traveling, pick up pillowcases (or fabrics to make your own) and take home a memory. Whether you select velvet, faux fur, suede, jacquard, silk blend, or cotton, your choices add to your home's visual appeal.

Sheepskin throws are inexpensive and add a soft, nubby texture to any space, whether they are draped over a sofa or chair or layered over an area rug in the bedroom.

Bring some texture upward with **wall hangings.** They are a softer, homey alternative to formal or contemporary artwork.

Room by Room

Textiles make a house a home in endless ways. Expressing yourself with fabrics in key spaces gives your home a distinct personality.

The Bedroom

This room is *all* about fabrics. Here, you create a nest where you relax, recharge, and rest easy. Textiles are the easiest way to make an impact quickly without a costly commitment.

Your Bed, Layer by Layer

Sure, textiles are found on your walls, floor, and loveseat, but let's get in bed together. My bed is my resting place, my sanctuary. It's where I return every night and where I linger on Sunday morning. I like to mix fabrics. My sheets are percale, my duvet cover is linen, and I like a quilt on top for how it looks and the extra weight. Usually there are six to eight pillows on my bed, though some end up stacked on a chair when I sleep. I like the versatility and the choice of different firmnesses from moment to moment. You might feel more minimalist.

Your bed is so personal that no one can tell you how to style it but you. I *can* tell you that this is the place to indulge. Given how close these fabrics are to your skin, and how much time you are spending on and under them, they are worth a solid investment. The bed is the most intimate part of your home, so treat it with kindness and care. Before deciding on bedding, ask yourself these questions:

What is my preferred feel?

What feels good on your skin? Think about this before you select color or pattern. Touching different bedding fabrics is paramount to knowing what will provide the comfort you seek.

What is my sleep style?

Do you run hot or cold when you sleep? If it's the former, choose a fabric that has optimal breathability, and is naturally cool to the touch, like percale. Also consider the climate where you live. If it's humid, linen is a smart pick because it's exceptionally breathable. If you like to feel snuggled up, sateen and its smooth, lustrous finish is a good choice for you.

Sheets

I gravitate toward bedding made with natural fibers, like cotton and linen. Using high-quality material allows for longevity, and the handfeel gets softer over time. From there, you can pick the weave that fits your personal profile. The sensation of sheets against your skin can impact your sleep experience. These are my favorites among all the many options:

Percale, made from cotton, has a cool, crisp, and clean feel. It is comparable to the perfect white button-down: It has a matte finish, is breathable and lightweight, and is perfect for all seasons.

Sateen, also made from cotton, uses a different weave than percale. It has a lustrous look and almost satin-like drape that feels warmer against your skin. It's ultrasmooth and luxurious. As a bonus, sateen is naturally more wrinkle-resistant for a sumptuous, inviting bed.

Linen is made from flax; its looser weave makes it breathable and durable. If you like a laid-back look, but enjoy the feel of luxury, this is a great choice whether you run warm or cool. The handfeel gets softer over time.

Covers

The various types of bed covers have distinct differences. Know what they are in order to make your bedroom feel like your sanctuary.

A **duvet** cover protects your down or alternate-fill insert while keeping

The sensation of sheets against your skin can impact your sleep experience.

Bedding Labels: What You Need to Know

Thread Count

Fact: Thread count is the number of threads woven into one square inch of fabric. With bedding, that number maxes out at around 400, because only so many pieces of thread can fit into a specific space. It's not the count, but the quality and type of threads that really matter. By keeping the thread count number lower and using premium fibers, the quality is maintained over time.

Fluff: Many manufacturers employ creative and somewhat deceptive math to market 1,000-plus thread counts. Threads in a fabric are single-ply (single strands twisted together) or two- or three-ply (multiple strands twisted together). If each thread is counted separately, or thinner threads are used to increase the count, numbers go up. Then, to restore a better feel, synthetic finishes are added. This approach compromises the fabric's softness, comfort, and quality. Some "higher" thread counts are actually heavier sheets that feel stiff and don't breathe well.

Certification

Fact: An Oeko-Tex certification means the fabric contains no harmful substances and conforms to a stringent set of guidelines at every stage of production—all to protect both the bedding and you.

Fluff: Fibers grown organically—but processed with toxic chemicals—may still carry the organic label, but they aren't certified. "Wrinkle free" or "permanent press" labels should be avoided because the fabrics are treated with formaldehyde resin, a toxic chemical.

Fill Power

Fact: Fill power or loft is a measurement of how fluffy the down is inside a duvet or pillow insert. The number represents how many cubic inches one ounce of down fills when at maximum loft or fluffiness. The higher the number, the better quality the down.

Fluff: Fill power is not a measure of firmness, weight, or heaviness. A 750 fill down feather duvet is not firmer than lower numbers; it is fluffier and warmer.

you cozy. Changing duvet covers is an easy way to get a new look each season or whenever you feel like it. I personally love a linen duvet because it adds just the right amount of texture; find what works best for you.

TIP A quick note about **duvet inserts**. Look for those with baffle box construction where the insert is sewn with squares or pockets to hold the filling in place. It minimizes the movement of fill to avoid clumping and keeps it evenly distributed for a light, airy experience. Inserts come in different weights.

Quilts add pattern and texture. Drape one at the foot of your bed for easy access, or use one on its own during warmer months. The weight comes from batting stitched between two outer layers; a medium weight is ideal for layering. I like a modern box-pattern quilt—the one I have is linen on one side and cotton percale on the other, giving me the option of using it two ways.

If you prefer a lighter weight with less batting, choose a **coverlet.** This is a lightweight decorative bedcover good for adding a finished look or layering for moderate extra warmth.

I use **throws** more decoratively. I like to have them at arm's reach at the foot of my bed, folded in the closet, or in a basket. I drape one over my shoulders while reading in bed. Throws add both extra warmth and decoration. The fabrics may change with the seasons, but whichever I have around—linen, cashmere, or alpaca—they always complete the look.

Pillows and Shams

What finishing touches give your bed a signature look?

Sleeping pillows come in soft, medium, or firm fill and should have a 100 percent cotton shell for comfort and breathability. Back sleepers usually prefer a medium fill to support their necks. Stomach sleepers use a soft pillow to keep their necks in a neutral position. And side sleepers typically use firm. Down pillows are supportive and durable with a fluffy, light feel. If you have allergies, a microfiber or other down alternative is best. These will be dressed like the rest of your bedding.

Shams are decorative pillowcases. They can be accented with color, pattern, or details like a flange, edging, or stitching. Two standard shams fit on a queen-size bed; three on a king-size bed. Two king shams fit on a king-size bed. A Euro sham is a true square shape and can mix and match with the other styles. On my bed, I layer quilted cotton shams and linen Euro shams. Mixing fabrics and textures adds depth, dimension, and interest.

Whatever the size and shape, select textiles that you enjoy and appreciate seeing daily. Pillows add the finishing touch to your nesting spot.

A Change of Season

A change in the weather is always an opportunity to rejuvenate your bedroom. Each season invites a fresh bedding set to wrap you in the perfect feel. In winter I gravitate to darker colors, use heavier throws, and dress my bed in layers of sheets, quilts, and duvets. Come spring, I trade my alpaca throw for lighter-weight linen and change my heavier bedroom quilt for an airy cotton one. In summer, cotton throws, sisal rugs, and linen bedding are easy swaps. I focus on what I can change easily rather than more permanent textiles like a rug or wall hanging.

Your Bedroom Is More Than Your Bed

If you have room for a cozy chair, a chaise lounge, an end-of-bed bench, or a vanity and stool, extend your textile selections to continue the warmth of what's on your bed. To complement a neutral and solid bed, these additional textiles can be more dramatic with patterns, embroidery, needlepoint, or vintage looks. This furniture is where you can add more dramatic tones or touches. Do keep your choices within the theme of a bedroom, though—soft, inviting, comfortable, pleasing to the eye.

The Bath

Even this smallest room should be lovely and welcoming. You have a range of options and can draw upon your cleverness and creativity. Taking time for your most private room can have a big payoff—visually, physically, and emotionally.

Towels

Start with towels. After all, the only good reason to leave a warm shower or bath is to wrap yourself in a dreamy towel. Quality material is paramount, so always **choose 100 percent cotton.** Turkish cotton is considered the best. It has a long heritage, and the fabric produced in the region is as soft, absorbent, and durable as it gets. I want every towel to feel like a luxurious 5-star hotel experience.

You definitely want towels that absorb well and are soft and quick to dry. Towels embrace you, so indulge here. Go for a fresh set in a color that feels soothing to you. Since they are laundered often and absorb soaps and body lotions that can cause discoloration, towels require replacement more frequently than other textiles in your home.

So, which kinds of towels? Know your options.

A good place to start is with a set of looped **terry bath towels** in white or a neutral shade. They work with any design and instantly evoke a calm, spa-like feeling.

Turkish towels, made from Turkish cotton, are thinner and lighter, great for the beach.

Fouta towels have a different feel; they feature tightly woven cotton on one side and plush cotton terry on the other. Thanks to this unique composition, these towels maintain superior absorbency and softness while being lightweight.

Waffle towels have a honeycomb weave and a minimalist, modern vibe. It's no wonder you see them in so many high-end hotels and spas.

Many people are perplexed about the right mix of sizes or what makes a good set. You can't go wrong. I suggest getting four to six standard **bath towels** or **bath sheets,** which are oversized. I normally go with standard towels as the sheets are a bit big for me. Add the same number (or more, if you like) of **hand towels** and **washcloths.** Even if you don't use them, they are good to have for guests.

TIP Order a few black 100 percent cotton towels for removing your makeup at night. This protects your regular towels from stains.

Bath Mats and Rugs

Bath mats and rugs are a necessity to avoid the odd chance of a slip and fall after a bath or shower. That said, my main reason for having one is keeping my feet nice and warm. And on the occasion that I am applying makeup or face cream and an item slips from my hand, having a cushiony surface on the hard floor can prevent breakage—a smart preventive solution.

A bath mat usually has a tight weave and dense loops and is an extension of the towel family. These are typically placed just outside of the shower or bath.

Bath rugs add a decorative element, while still being soft, absorbent, and warm underfoot. Choices abound: contrasting weave, stripes, chunky yarns with tassels, and colors that complement your towels or your bathroom color design. You might have two of different sizes—one tub size and one long runner fit for a Jack and Jill sink.

My choice is always 100 percent cotton for the best absorption and fastest drying time. Even in a guest bathroom sans shower, a bath rug can add a finishing touch and a bit of cushion, particularly if you have tile flooring.

Any time you purchase a floor covering, even for the bathroom, be sure to measure. I have had the occasion of purchasing a rug only to find it didn't lay flat in the allotted space. Consider that bathroom rug sizes are typically 20 to 24 inches wide and 30 to 36 inches long.

Whatever is placed in front of your shower or bath will accumulate moisture. When not in use, hang it on a rod or the side of your tub to air-dry it more quickly and completely. A bath rug by the sink does not work as hard. Bath mats require washing with the frequency of your towels; bath rugs can be less frequent—weekly or bi-weekly. If a bathroom toilet rug is part of your décor, wash it the most often.

Shower Curtains

Another element that adds a finishing touch to the bathroom is the shower curtain. Once upon a time, shower curtains were all waterproof drapes, so to speak. Now by having a shower curtain liner (mildew resistant and completely waterproof), you can choose an attractive curtain that adds to the design and style of your bath.

The choices are extensive. You can select a beautiful minimalist curtain that accents the walls and towels or go for a more dramatic selection that is the centerpiece. Do you have bath rugs with tassels? Select a shower curtain with tassels for a complete look. Or if the bathroom and towels are all solid colors, horizontal lines on a white shower curtain can add a distinct contrast.

Even the small functional details offer a chance for style. I prefer modern "S" stainless-steel shower curtain rings for just the right accent.

Robes

I'm a firm believer that a cozy, luxurious robe is the perfect way to start and end a day. A robe is the ultimate relaxation wear. Why hide it? Place a hook in your bathroom for this luxury item and have it always at the ready.

With an item this essential, I find one does not suffice. Different seasons require different-weight robes. I have a classic terry robe with a snug, cozy collar as my basic plush relaxation wear for winter. As the warmer weather arrives, I switch to a lighter weight, either a waffle fabric robe or an airy cotton one. All must have pockets.

When you find the right robe (or robes) for yourself, indulge a bit. Comfort matters, and your robe is another sign of making home a place of comfort that's just right for you.

The Kitchen and Dining Room

Food preparation, serving, and eating are filled with textured moments, centered in both the kitchen and dining areas.

In my first apartment, I used disposable items and my dishcloths doubled as potholders. Several burned tables and hands later, I began to appreciate the design and aesthetic of such household goods. I found that different fibers made certain purchases better investments and I reduced waste, which is an environmental plus. My kitchen now is still small; I don't have room for excess, so **four potholders,** a set of **napkins for eight,** and **six well-used dishcloths** suffice. Additional items are in marked bins in the garage so I can easily grab what I need when I have more people over for dinner or when it's time to replace a dishcloth that has expired. These textiles make me feel at home because they allow me to easily accomplish what I want to in this all-important central room of my house.

Invest in more than one tablecloth or set of placemats. You can easily swap out linens to make your dining area read more formal and thematic or more fun and whimsical. Layering these items—like a patterned square tablecloth over a longer solid linen cloth—is unexpected and adds dimension. Or use a **table runner** on its own for a minimalist touch that goes a long way—pun intended.

An **apron** is always a yes for me; something about tying one on really brings me into the space and the experience of cooking.

An **area rug** in the kitchen is my most recent addition. It looks good, and there are certain versions that make it easier on the body to stand and prepare food for an hour or so. And at the pet store I found a mat especially for my dog, so my floor is protected from spills from her bowls. Plus I like to think she knows that space is specially designated for her.

When you're choosing fabrics for dining room chairs or a bench in a dining nook, be sure the fabric can be wiped clean easily and does not absorb stains or smells.

The Living Room

Some rooms—like the bath and kitchen—have textiles that are purpose-made. Living rooms are more varied. Some are spacious with high ceilings, others are intimate and double as a den or dining room. One thing that holds consistent is how textiles add interest and comfort. This is the space you share most with friends and family, so create a room that invites everyone to linger. While the furniture sets the structure, the

textiles do the heaviest lifting here—the majority of items in the living room are covered with fabrics. The living room is dense with choices.

I spent the most time designing my living room because it's where you can usually find me. It serves so many purposes: relaxing, hosting, casual just-us dinners, the occasional dance party, movie night. When purchasing my first couch, I was amazed as I educated myself on the myriad textile options out there. And my excitement continued when I was selecting pillows, curtains, and other decorative pieces. It was eye-opening.

As you are collecting or adjusting all the moving parts, focus on the idea of **cohesion.** A living room can easily hold a mix of textiles. Part of the reason I gravitate toward neutral colors for my couch and rugs is that they're a reliable foundation and a perfect backdrop. Select your showcase fabrics deliberately (see page 93 for more on different types).

Attention to the size and proportion of textiles in the room helps with **balance.** Several twill and solid pillows strewn on the couch can look attractive, but too many can look off-kilter. Once your larger pieces—curtains, rugs, sofa, chairs—are set, experiment with your movable pieces to find what feels right to you.

Do you sense that **something is missing?** Because I am drawn to textural elements and fabrics of all kinds, I notice when they are absent and a space is lacking a certain something. It's more of a feeling I get in a room than a textbook idea. When I sense an area could use a little more—an additional embroidered pillow on a loveseat, an area rug under a coffee table, an oversized floor cushion in a corner—I repurpose items from other rooms to experiment and discover what completes the look.

Mix and match often. Soft goods counteract hard surfaces or edges. Think of how a cozy wool throw softens the shine of a leather couch. Make an assessment of the textures already in your space. If you have wicker furniture, you might want to think about layering in some smoother textures. If a space is filled with harder, glossier surfaces, try looser, raw finishes for warmth.

5

ACCENTUATE THE PERSONAL

When putting on the final touches, showcase the pieces and accessories you love that ultimately set your home apart. As you find, curate, and arrange accents, these more intimate touches will tell your story.

When you get dressed in the morning, you put on an outfit and then you add a jacket, jewelry, a scarf, or a headband. These are the touches that personalize your look. Selecting artwork, decorative furniture, mirrors, and other accessories is also personal. My home is a visual collection of mementos from my travels, photos with family, a favorite coffee table book, keepsakes from my wedding, a bowl from my grandmother, an impulse buy at an antiques fair, and so much other inspiration.

As I walk through my home, different rooms hold different elements of my experiences. My bedroom has minimal accessories—a bedside table catchall for jewelry, a wall hanging from a flea market, two art pieces made by a friend. When cooking, I grab a pinch of salt from a ceramic bowl, and I recall a stall in

Mexico City. I spotted the long bench in my entryway at a shop in Soho; it's multipurpose, showcasing a photo of downtown L.A., an occasional stack of books, and is often where I stash my sunglasses. The metal sculpture I found in Santa Barbara is the ideal topper on a stack of books. I accessorize my baby's room with a piggy bank and favorite books from my childhood, my daughter's favorite stuffed airplane, bunnies, and pink dinosaur, and with a wooden mobile of varied shapes that is light and airy.

Enjoy this form of expression that is uniquely you; it is how you truly nest. Here, in choosing what you have and how it is presented, it's fine to abandon practicality. Don't overthink; eliminate the rules. Be playful and expressive. Accentuate your home with whatever evokes positive memories and brings you joy each day.

How Do Accents Make a House a Home?

When I moved into this house, I made an artificial deadline of a housewarming party to hold myself accountable for unpacking boxes and getting art on the walls. Once the furniture was all in place, the house was "set up," but it lacked character. Those extra elements do more than convey an aesthetic. If furniture is the bones of the room, the accents are the soul. They allow you to reflect what you are passionate about, and to surround yourself with what you want to see every day. This tapestry of elements can change—either rarely or often—so be okay with switching things up and bringing out something special for an occasion to remember. I look forward to these continual changes. Your story is always in process; let your home evolve with you.

How do I start?

Select one room and remove all the accessories. Check that you have the furniture in the best locations, then slowly add in pieces to see what works. You might decide a side table is best topped with one item rather than six. A cluster of three small potted plants may sit well on a low bench. Objects can be placed on top of books to add height. Set the scene, step back, and admire or adjust.

How much variety can I have?

As much as you want! But with a note of caution: Too much of a good idea can become an overstatement and dominate the design in the room. If that's your look, go for it—but harmony can come from variety. Integrate items that feel trendy and "of the moment" sparingly. Avoid a theme; for example, if everything is shells and anchors, the nautical look can get tired quickly. A round side table may work on one side of the couch with a lower square table easing into the corner on the other side. Place a vintage metal teapot on the bar by the painted shot glasses from Mexico, alongside the animal chopstick holders from China. Accessorizing does not have to be permanent.

What creates a sense of balance?

Balance does not always mean "even." Clustering accessories in odd numbers rather than even groupings helps avoid an appearance of a staged vignette. Try placing three items on one side table and a single one on the other. Then look from different angles to see what you like. Experiment with moving items of different heights forward and back on a shelf to see what pleases your eye. Color can give your composition coherence, whether you're using a single color or many.

The Art of Layering

A thoughtful home is filled with intentionality: You add and subtract items to reach your desired look and feel. By dressing your home in layers, you achieve an integrated look while still allowing something to pop with distinction. Why does this matter? Effective layering contributes to the overall flow and brings out the best in your paint colors, wallpaper, flooring, textiles, and lighting. All of these factors combine as you continue to contemplate what you can add or adjust to truly make yourself at home.

Inspiration Everywhere

The accents throughout my house are a road map of my journey, my life. Collectively, they speak to where I have come from, where I have been, and where I am going next. That's why I separate them into distinct buckets: what I already have, what I seek out and choose, and unexpected attractions. All three categories are of equal importance, and they blend to tell a richer, more fascinating story of my home and me.

Family History

Heirlooms and photographs provide the most personal touches to your home. They take on new meaning in this context, adding to the value they carry from their original time and place. I love to decorate with family photos, especially mixing them in with other assorted pieces of art—a landscape photograph, an abstract drawing, or an oil painting. If you have a collection of photos you want to display, consider removing them from their original frames and unifying them in a grid, or in modern white or black frames.

Spread the items you've inherited around your space, which will keep your home from looking dated or like a mini-museum. With furniture pieces like a great-aunt's dining room set, remember it's okay to mix it up. Most design today is less about matching sets and more about mixing pieces together to form a new heirloom story. You don't need to re-create your relative's space, but rather, you can take advantage of the opportunity to honor their pieces in your space. That elegant solid-walnut table could be paired with a set of sleek bentwood or mid-century chairs. The same concept applies to all the items you inherit: Those brass candlesticks may look fantastic acting as bookends on your shelf.

These types of artifacts bring desired memories into my home; I personally find them nourishing. At the same time, I have found myself in a quandary when I feel "done" with a hand-me-down table or painting. My advice is to lovingly let go. Make room when you want a new look, a change, or something else appealing to your evolving preferences.

Shopping at Home

Before investing in pieces you want or need, shop your own home. Just like you can shorten a long dress for a whole new look, look around and see what could be repurposed in a different spot, or another room altogether. Moving a sculpture from a bedroom shelf to a living room coffee table can be surprisingly transformative. A vintage plate that you never unpacked could sit well on the mantel. A piece of art might simply need a new frame to achieve the exact look you want in the dining room.

Sometimes you just need a fresh pair of eyes, so grab your friend who finds the best goodies at flea markets and see what can be discovered in your home. This is also a way to get rid of excess: If you aren't using it, if you don't love it, if you don't see the possibility for using it later, and if the dominant thought is "Why do I have this?," then clear it out! Make room for something new, or for a purposefully unadorned, calming space that might have been the answer all along.

Travel

Think of the adventures you have in new places; do you want to bring them home with you? The memory of watching ceramic bowls being painted in Istanbul comes back every time I see those bowls on my shelf. These treasures bring character to your home, and reflect an appreciation of other cultures. When you're traveling, avoid tourist shops and seek out local artisans who capture the country's aesthetics and history, and who carry on local traditions. Block out time to explore. Your purchases will invite conversation and stories, and help you keep the feeling of the journey present even after you're back home. In decorating, try mixing these with cherished photos to personalize even further.

Instinctual Buys

A designer once told me if you see something in a shop that you really love, you should just get it—don't worry too much if it goes with other things you have. Through the years, I have found this advice

to be solid. If you truly love something, it is right—period. This is my guiding principle when I am shopping and find myself drawn to a piece; I focus on how it makes me feel. A few of my favorite objects were impulse purchases: a large woven basket, a metal plant stand, a large classroom chalkboard. If you feel a connection, you will find a place in your home for an instinctual buy even if it takes a while. It belongs because it is something that sparked joy in you.

Strong Statements

A strong statement doesn't have to be an assault. It is just another way to express who you are, and one that adds interest, excitement, maybe a bit of surprise. It's tied to what you like, what feels comfortable, or what pushes you beyond your comfort zone.

When finding your statement piece, play—play with shape, color, size, and proportion. Extend yourself in new directions. You might discover it becomes an anchor in a room, or it may be a special standout that adds a missing element at the end of the design process. You may find a vintage coffee table carved from driftwood that becomes a centerpiece, or a hand-dyed geometric wall hanging that lifts your view.

Perhaps your statement piece reflects *wabi-sabi*, the Japanese concept of perfection in imperfection. This traditional aesthetic celebrates the idea of beauty that is imperfect, impermanent, and incomplete. It could mean a piece of pottery that has a rough finish over a smooth one, or a lamp base that is somewhat asymmetrical. I am drawn to these types of pieces because they look like they tell a more personal story or catch the eye in a different way—they have a natural authenticity.

Decorative Furniture

Your foundational pieces—like the sofa, bed, dresser, and dining table—are larger investments in your home. Because they command a considerable part of your space and budget, think of them as timeless. With some exceptions, they tend to be neutral in color and shape, which gives you the opportunity to add decorative pieces like chairs, side tables, lamps, and other accents that can add nuance and character.

Seating choices encourage conversation, and tend to express your style of entertaining. You can choose from mid-century modern to French ornate, overstuffed upholstery to simple Shaker-style walnut. To convey calmness and serenity, select linear, slim profiles and shades of white, cream, and beige. For a more whimsical feeling, look for curvy backs and arms and colorful fabric. If you and your guests are loungers, think about more forgiving shapes and larger silhouettes that encourage people to get comfortable and stay awhile.

Ottomans and **poufs** are handy and take up little space. Smaller and softer than chairs, they are great in a kid's room, or make an instant table when topped with a tray.

I favor a **bench** because it supplies architectural lines and is versatile. It can be a bonus surface at the end of a bed, a bookshelf in the living room, or extra seating in a dining room.

Coffee tables need to hold many items, from magazines to coffee cups to remote controls. They can have personality alongside function. Choose **glass or clear acrylic** for an airy look and feel, **dark, rich wood** for a formal, library look, or **metal** if you know the area will get a lot of wear and tear. **Light wood** is a sure thing in almost any space.

Side tables vary as well. A unique shape or particularly delicate version can stand on its own as an art piece. I've used one in lieu of a nightstand, another as a plant stand, and paired two to replace a coffee table. They can match or not; I tend to lean toward "or not," with the exception of my bedroom nightstands.

With their slim, sleek profiles, **consoles** maximize your space to display personal items like collections, books, and artwork, or additional lighting. They can be strictly decorative or have cabinetry for storage. If you need a small, narrow counter in your entryway, a console is a great option.

I had not planned on a **bar cart** until I received one as a gift. Now I am a believer. There is a definite advantage to having attractive glassware and bottles at the ready. This stand-alone piece also gives me a display area for a few favorite items, like a tall vase with branches and a piece of crystal.

Bookshelves add flavor to common rooms. They combine function with style. You can choose from many looks: floor-to-ceiling, cabinet, wall-mounted, a corner unit—just to name a few. The materials are equally diverse. Bookshelves give you the canvas to display many of the finishing touches discussed in this chapter, making them an integral part of being home.

Artwork

Paintings, sculptures, drawings, and photographs all add a sense of creativity and liveliness. What you are attracted to, and what you want to be surrounded by, says a lot about who you are and what you love. But it's easy to get complacent and fall into a rut where you keep choosing the same types of art. So go to a museum or local gallery to expose yourself to today's emerging artists. What you display should be as varied and unique as you.

Mix up your mediums (or don't)

A series of graphic prints in white frames will look ordered and modern. If you want a more relaxed mélange of visuals, then pull together old photos, graphic posters, sketches, and black-and-white photography, along with several three-dimensional objects.

Use it unexpectedly

Hang an oversized piece that comforts you behind your bed. Combine artwork with a chair and side table to create a nook or vignette for yourself. If you lack a window, use a piece of art to mimic an outdoor scene and take in the view.

It doesn't have to hang

Leaning framed art on a ledge like a low bench, on the floor, on a chair, a low bookshelf, or a higher piece like a dresser or console is often unexpected, but it really can work and add another dimension. The look is a bit more relaxed, and as a bonus, allows you to move the pieces around anytime you like. Additional perks are no lingering nail holes, plus you might be able to hide things like stray wires and unsightly outlets. Create an artist's loft vibe by using a shallow ledge or floating shelf to display your favorite artwork or photography. Fill the

Tips to Create a Gallery Wall

I knew I wanted an eye-catching gallery wall in my living room. Curating it allowed me to put my creativity and joy on high volume, and turn an ordinary wall of decent art into a unique collection of my very favorite visuals. I usually have fourteen pieces making up my assortment of paintings, photos, paper art, and a signed album cover, and predictably, guests linger here to see their favorites and check out what's new. It is a full and public display of *me*.

Pick one piece to take center stage
Typically, this is your most substantial piece. If you have multiple large pieces, start by centering them.

Arrange carefully
I suggest you lay out the gallery wall on the floor to consider spacing and story before you hammer your first nail. Play here. Rearrange until it feels right to you. Pick an approach: Either create a cohesive look with art placed as one larger statement (allow two inches of space between each piece), or spread the items out for a more expansive look and feel.

Balance the bold
If you have a bright blue piece on the right side, find artwork that has a blue accent for the left side, otherwise your eye will only see the boldest piece, overlooking the others. Keep the darkest and heaviest artwork near the bottom.

Create shape
Gallery walls look best if they have pieces of varying widths and heights. Create a rhombus or pentagon shape, so artwork at the peaks of the cluster sits highest.

Continue to move things around
This part takes time. You might create thirty different combinations until one feels right. If you like a particular arrangement but want to try a few more, snap a picture so you can go back to it later.

empty space of a nonworking fireplace with a framed photo, sketch, or painting. Dot small spaces with other objects. Place a treasured piece on an artist's easel to make it the center of attention.

Mirrors

Mirrors have obvious practical uses, but they can also be artful visuals in a room. With so much variation in frames, there's a mirror for every space and vice versa. You can use a mirror like another window; the reflection can double the outside view. Placed strategically, the reflection can enhance a piece of art or a grouping of decorative accents. Hang a mirror above a striking piece of furniture or mantel to highlight the feature without overwhelming or distracting. A collection of mirrors allows light to bounce around the space. And mirrors also capture and reflect any bit of natural and artificial light (see page 81). I personally love a mirror somewhere unexpected like an oversized or ornate mirror above a stove or propped against a wall at the end of a dining room table.

Books

Books are deeply personal. They reveal what we enjoy, what transports us, and what inspires us. They add immediate warmth. I always enjoy perusing a friend's bookshelf to discover other aspects of who they are.

Books also add color, pattern, and shape depending on how they are stacked, shelved, or displayed. Use them as a design element in any space, such as in a **composed grid** on a coffee table. In this instance, choose larger editions with visually compelling covers, like those with eye-catching graphics or photography.

You can also use them to **elevate an object** by stacking three or four books and topping them with an accent piece like a vase or sculpture. This trick can add height and balance where needed.

Color-coordinating your books on a built-in or standing bookcase will give the space a playful bespoke look. If you don't have enough of each color, consider purchasing books by color at a library sale. The design itself becomes a piece of art that is pleasing to the eye.

Be Flexible

Adaptability is key to creating a home that moves and shifts with you as your home grows and changes. These are some of my favorite ways to build flexible spaces.

Double-Duty Furniture
Invest in some quick-change artists to increase your design options.
Drop-leaf tables can be a dining area or an active entry piece
Ottomans are extra seating or an impromptu cocktail table (just add a tray)
Daybeds are a cozy reading nook by day and a guest room by night
A **slim bench** against the wall can be pulled out for dining seats

Space-Saving Accessories
In tight quarters, every square inch counts.
Wall sconces free up surface area so no lamp is needed in a tight entry or bedroom
A **backless bookshelf** can become a room divider; fill it with favorite things while still letting the light through
Wallpaper is a chic headboard as an alternative to a proper bed frame
A **deep, wide dresser** can store linens if you lack closet space

One Room Becomes Two
If you don't have a dedicated room to meet your needs, consider how you can diversify the use of space.
Place both a **desk** and a small **sofa** in an extra room to make a hybrid office/kids' hangout
A **slim, round table** in a living room corner displays books and objects by day and makes a cozy dinner spot
An unused **space under the stairs** may double as a mini-office and a snug place for a book nook

Leave intriguing **books opened** on a side table, coffee table, or console. They will inspire you each time you pass by, or encourage guests to flip through them.

Use books as a **side table.** Stack a pile of your sturdiest, largest books up to side table height (around 25 inches) and top them with a tray. This is an unpredictable (and low-cost) way to have a table, and it's full of much more personality than anything you'll find in a store.

Mix books in with other objects on your shelves for visual interest. Variety is always pleasing to the eye and allows for a collection of several items to tell a story.

Vary the placement of your books. Place some books standing up side by side, and stack others horizontally. Turn some so that the spines are facing in, or flip one upside down to see if anyone notices your secret. Create pockets to add in other items that will stand out in this linear arrangement.

Finishing Touches
Small pieces are what finish off a space and complete your signature style. Maybe you brought back cherished crystals from a recent wellness adventure, or you picked up a perfect figurine on a trip. Use these and other treasures as punctuation marks to draw the eye, to add color, or as a shiny object for reflection.

Trays corral smaller items and bring order and calm to a shelf, table, or counter.

Candles and candlesticks add mood lighting anytime, for a dinner party of two or twenty. They lend height, sculptural interest, and reflective sheen in the form of brass, silver, gold, glass, and certain ceramics.

Vases can be displayed with or without flowers or foliage. They add hits of color on a table or on a shelf. Group several sizes and shapes together for artful impact.

Bowls can be used in and out of the kitchen, and do more than hold odds and ends. No matter their material, they add a curvy shape and look eye-catching in groups or in a bigger size.

Smaller sculptural pieces bring interest to side tables, shelves, and coffee tables, and bring contrast, color, and whimsy anywhere you place them. Whether playful or serious—a little ceramic house you picked up in Amsterdam, a miniature carved bust from a local artist, a pair of metal frogs—they draw the eye and represent *you*.

TIP Leave space around items to allow your eye to rest every so often. No matter how stunning, visuals quickly become chaotic if there is no calm space in between.

6

MAKE SOME SPACE

Eliminating clutter transforms your home into a place with purpose. Every item belongs somewhere for a reason. By removing distraction and excess, we lighten up, creating room for wellness and joy.

When I rid myself of physical clutter, amazingly, I clear mental clutter at the same time. Have you ever noticed that cleaning out your closet just makes you feel better overall? It's like working out—I never regret it! I am certain that being organized at home has been essential for my personal harmony and balance.

I can exist in a state of clutter for only so long. One weekend during my annual spring-cleaning binge, I tossed an unidentified phone charger into a drawer with other misplaced items. Then I had an aha moment: I pulled out all the items stuffed into a "miscellaneous" bin under the bed, swept the "I-don't-know-where-these-go" things off the shelf, emptied the aforementioned junk drawer, and made a firm decision to shift my intention.

I transitioned from a mind-set of clearing out unused and unloved items and surface cleaning routines to finding a broader system of organization to suit my long-term mission of making a peaceful and harmonious home. I sought out tools that could help me live better on a daily basis so that I am always greeted by a welcoming environment after a day out at work, and so that I don't have to go into a cleaning frenzy when guests are coming. Everyday organization equals everyday balance.

How Does Organizing Make a House a Home?

Everyone has a different tolerance for "stuff." Tidiness doesn't have to be about clearing away everything except the essentials. Instead, let it be about figuring out how your home helps you work efficiently, enjoy your space, and welcome others in.

A clutter-free, organized home requires more than just clearing the counters or straightening up a drawer. What we have around us links directly to how we feel and function. For me, less clutter reduces my stress and makes me feel good. It's tougher for me to enjoy my home when it is in disarray. When I'm consistent with organizing my home, this concept isn't daunting. I'm glad to tidy up; it's easier. I want to be here.

A thoughtful place for everything in your home means that some things are on full display for you to enjoy or grab, others are tucked away in a closet or drawer with easy access, and the rest is stored for a future time and place in the garage or attic. Whether you are a minimalist or maximalist, this simple idea of clarifying what goes where makes your home more functional.

I want every item to have a place in my home. I ask myself three questions to create three essential categories that guide me in knowing what belongs where:

What do I use every day?
Clothing, kitchenware, work essentials, dog leashes, keys, mail, select cookbooks, reusable shopping bags

What do I use weekly?

Vacuum cleaner, waffle maker, artsy books I peruse for inspiration, picnic blankets, vase, candlesticks, yoga mat

What do I use a few times a year?

Champagne flutes, an oversized platter, card table, large suitcase, a board game

These are just my answers; think about yours. If you have items that don't make it into any of these categories, consider repurposing, donating, or discarding them in the most responsible way.

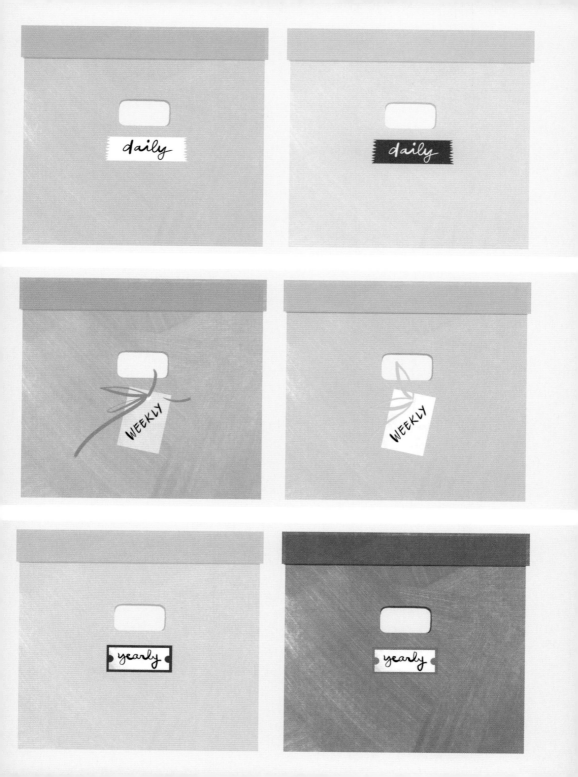

Make a System

Once everything is sorted, you can prioritize what remains at your fingertips, what is stashed for easy access, and what gets stored away. When you have a reliable system, you can defer to it again and again and keep your home arranged in the way that works for you. Go old-school with paper and pen; keep a ledger or journal that you can refer to and adapt as you develop your approach. When I made time for this exercise, what had seemed a bit overwhelming became manageable— and the payoff was huge: I had a record of out-of-sight items and I could see and appreciate what I had close by. And I found that places that needed an extra touch, like a bouquet of flowers, became apparent. Decluttering brings relief with tangible visible benefits. My home was lighter and brighter.

Stowaways

Getting rid of clutter and storing what I did not readily need was life-changing. Putting things away is only one perk—the other is being able to find them.

Seasonal items are things you do not need daily, weekly, or even monthly. They may be tied to weather, celebrations, and holidays, like the heavy throws that come out in October, a thematic tablecloth for the Fourth of July, or maracas for Cinco de Mayo. They have importance for a discrete period of time.

Gather your seasonals, sort them into bins, and put them somewhere out of sight. I use my garage to organize and store these items. You can also use a basement, attic, or even a guest room closet. Small spaces work, too: I keep my dog's Halloween costume on the top closet shelf

I want every item
to have a place in
my home.

behind my winter boots. Label them for easy identification and record them in your journal for a backup.

Opening my linen closet and not seeing picnic supplies or holiday decorations stashed next to my washcloths is a relief. And now I am delighted to retrieve them when the time comes, as a mark of transition from one season to the next. Clearing out that closet also let me make it a more functional space to store my linens. It's a positive snowball effect.

Family heirlooms that aren't being displayed but that you still want to keep can also be stored away. I recently did this with some keepsake items from my wedding in Mexico. I don't want to toss the etched wood signs we used as decoration or a copy of the menu, but I have no need for them on a daily basis. They're treasures I know I can call on for a special family gathering or anniversary.

Off-season clothing and shoes are also great candidates for putting out of sight. Moving them frees up space in your drawers and closets and ultimately saves you time when you're looking for something. When I am running late for a meeting and can grab my beige sandals without riffling past knee-high boots, I eliminate last-minute frenzy.

Weekend or Occasional Items
With items you might use once or twice a week, create key storage areas in your home for easy access.

Games and puzzles can reside on a coffee table, if the boxes are particularly stylish, to encourage spontaneous play. I have a friend who collects vintage playing cards and keeps them in a chic bowl as an accent. If you have a large game collection, though, store them in a closet or console.

Stow **specialized cookware** in high cabinets or shelves that might otherwise sit empty. Why not use that space to store the Belgian waffle maker? Just remember to invest in a slim step stool so they are easy to reach when you need them. For items that are really

rarely used—a fondue set, perhaps—consider storing them outside of the kitchen.

TIP Books and magazines have a way of building up until you feel like they are a mountain about to bury you. Books—especially coffee table books—are designed to be picked up and put back down, but most magazines are disposable, so a stack of them can look like clutter. Sort through your collection and be discerning about what you hold on to and what you toss. I keep to a one-month approach: When the new issue arrives, the last one goes. This keeps me honest about reading the articles that matter most.

Corral **cleaning supplies** in an oversized bucket under the kitchen sink or in a taller bin stowed in a linen or hall closet. Either way, keep them together to be carted around room-to-room when you need them.

Everyday Essentials
You don't have to hide everything. For things you use every single day, be sure they are easily accessible, but in a way that's aesthetically pleasing.

In the Entry
A **tall glass cylinder or ceramic vase** holds umbrellas artfully, and helps keep your floors dry.

Your shoes will look better when kept on a **floor mat.**

A **small, decorative bowl or tray** distracts from a jumble of keys, loose change, or receipts.

Mail always looks less messy when it's in a **shallow tray or petite basket.**

In the Living Room
A **large woven basket** can hold spare throws of different weights for every season.

Assign a **drawer in your credenza** for remotes and a spare phone charger for guests.

Rearrange your pillows when you get off the couch so it looks fresh and ready for you.

Whatever you bring in that's not required, take out! Whether it's the novel you're reading on the sofa, or several coasters you were using with friends, return the items to where they belong.

In the Kitchen

If you want to keep pantry items like pasta, spices, or coffee out on the counter, use **clear glass jars** that either match or share a cohesive look.

Create an artisanal effect by using an **earthenware jug** to store wooden spoons and spatulas.

Open shelving encourages a display of mugs or specialty glassware in different sizes, colors, or shapes.

Consider a chef's kitchen look if you can't store all of your everyday items. Pots, pans, and dish towels can hang from a **rod with hooks.**

Similarly, a **magnetic strip or butcher's block** makes a great place for your most frequently used knives.

Inexpensive bamboo trays, shallow metal baskets, or clear bins or containers keep pantry shelves looking photo-ready.

Use a **bowl** on your countertop to hold fresh fruit—and to create a living still life.

Keep the insides of your **cupboards and drawers** neatly arranged, so your favorite serving items and most frequently used cookware, appliances, plates, stemware, and silverware are readily available. Invest in **dividers** for drawers to keep smaller items in their place.

In the Office

Make sure your desk or work surface is a clean slate to maximize productivity. Here, I would recommend being a minimalist. Leave room for your **computer** and other **true necessities,** and allow for a touch of the **personal**—a family photo, a small vase with flowers, or an inspiring card from your mentor. This is a place where everything must have a purpose: Only keep around what brings out the energy you need to do your work. If minimalism really is not your style, consider what would make your work area more manageable, then sort what you have into **folders, trays, or even curated piles** to find things more easily.

Tuck away all those extra cords, batteries, and any other tech accessories you don't need every day. **Use a basket or assign a drawer** for them.

Rid yourself of **digital clutter,** an unfortunate distraction. Go through files, delete the ones you no longer need, and then organize others into folders so you can access them quickly. While this may not improve your home directly, it can improve your psyche overall.

In the Bedroom

First and foremost, **make your bed.** Doing so each morning allows you to immediately check something off your list. By the time you get out of the shower, your room already looks welcoming and organized. This small act literally clears the space in the room and can help ground you. For me, it's a must-do morning ritual that I can manage even with limited time.

You have control over what you see before you sleep and what greets you when you open your eyes. So keep your nightstand free from anything

that makes you anxious, like a pile of books you've been meaning to read or unopened mail. Do have items that are useful and pleasing—a **small bowl** for your jewelry, a **lamp,** a **decanter of water** with a glass, **hand cream,** an **eye mask,** and a **favorite photo or object.** If it's your style, keep a **small journal** where you can empty your brain of a to-do list or whatever has you preoccupied, or where you can jot down three things you are grateful for before closing your eyes each night.

While being connected throughout the day via phone, tablet, or laptop can be productive, the blue light that screens emit can make it difficult to fall asleep. Calm your busy mind by **keeping devices out of your sleep space.** In fact, give yourself at least thirty minutes off technology before sleep to let it all go.

Whole books have been written on how to organize your clothing. But I want to share my brief primer on the organization that works best for me, and how it helps keep my bedroom homey.

Closets can be a slippery slope—one item out of place can quickly cascade into many, throwing off your whole balance. In a small closet, **categorizing by item type and color-coordinating** are the most helpful approaches. I arrange my long items together in this way, and then my shorter items. Placing my shoes in **plastic bins** was a game changer for me: I'm able to see my options and speedily choose what I need, plus the shoes don't get dusty. Purchase **narrow hangers** to save space and add **hooks** where you can for belts, ties, jackets, hats, and scarfs. I place items that can be rolled, like workout clothes, T-shirts, and pajamas, in **woven baskets** on shelves.

For drawers, I aim for simplicity with **clear dividers,** and I categorize, like I do in the closets. I have adopted the filing method of folding— Marie Kondo's **KonMari Method.** You can fit more in the drawers, and you can see all of your items. This is an especially huge plus for my baby's dresser, where I have limited space.

Once your system is in place, the greatest challenge is to make the time to roll and fold and hang all your clothes after the laundry is done or at day's end so you get back to "start" with a neatly arranged wardrobe. Instead of piling clothes on a chair, get in the habit of putting them in a **hamper** if they're dirty, or putting them back where they belong if not. This act is calming at the end of a long day, and reduces the visual clutter to help keep your bedroom a haven. And as a bonus, you're less likely to lose a sock.

In the Bath

Tackle your medicine cabinet, often a hot spot of clutter and chaos. Start by taking everything out and sorting by category—skin care, medicine, hair care, makeup. Arrange by these categories on the shelves. Place small, loose items like cotton pads or swabs in clear containers.

Do a **clean sweep of your vanity and sink area.** In a thoughtful fashion, tuck away anything you can in the medicine cabinet, a drawer, or a linen closet—be sure to put it in a clearly marked container, otherwise it just becomes more clutter. Then add a few **meaningful items** to personalize your space, like a small piece of decorative pottery for your jewelry, or handmade soap.

You can **store towels** in many ways, but I say *don't* hide them all in a closet. Instead, make a statement, whether you play with a mix of colors and finishes, or go ultraclean and composed with crisp white. I hang several from decorative hooks even in a small bathroom. For a guest bath, I like a straw or fabric basket with towels rolled neatly inside. Refer back to Chapter 4 on page 106 for more information on how these all-important textiles can help make your house a home.

7

TAKE CARE

A house gives you shelter. A home gives you a
sanctuary where you can relax and flourish. Home
is where you begin and end your day; you physically
and mentally recharge within these walls. Creating a
nourishing environment—for mind, body, and soul—is
an essential ingredient in your well-being.

nside my home, I need to create a place to retreat from the bigger picture of work and societal complexities. I depend on daily rituals that are personally soothing and comforting. Self-care is a must. Care for others—beings and things—gives me a sense of purpose.

I do my best at work and in my relationships when I *feel* my best. This effort starts in the morning before I even step out the door. And my home is also a haven when the day is over because I know comfort awaits when I can turn on my favorite music, take a warm shower, or inhale the scent of my latest floral arrangement. I can unwind and transition to relaxing; home is where my focus shifts. It helps me let go of outside stressors and feel cleansed from the day.

You might consider me a creature of habit. Within just a few weeks of moving into my house, I realized I kept sitting in the same spot on the couch and reaching for the same gray cashmere throw to wrap myself in after work. Evening sunsets in the backyard and playing catch with my dog became a regular part of my routine. I drank tea out of the same ceramic mug, going out of my way to be sure it was clean when I wanted it. I am a pretty simple person when it comes to what gives me comfort—but once I identified these routines, they became a cherished part of my time at home. Building on this idea of ritual, I have continued to figure out ways to intentionally add comfort and care for myself by having fresh flowers around the house, allowing empty space, keeping windows open, and more. My home and I are in constant conversation.

How Does Self-Care Make a House a Home?

You likely have a few favorite spots in your home. For me, they are the left end of the sofa, the easy chair in my daughter's room, and the long-cushioned bench at my outdoor table. After a busy day, one of these three spots is where I want to be.

We all have the retreats that are physically comfortable for us. There are places that are inspiring, where you can reach for a favorite book. And there are places you can snuggle into, that envelop you when you need to be held. A lot of this comfort comes from tiny touches that maybe only you notice. Being conscious of the parts of your home that conjure up positive and productive vibes allows you to make ongoing improvements. Here are questions to guide your journey toward a nurturing home:

What rituals have meaning for me?
Morning rituals can include drinking hot water with lemon when you wake up or sitting for a meditation before checking e-mails. You might find turning off the TV an hour before bed and reading a book instead becomes your calming, centering practice. Notice what you already do, and think about how it makes you feel. Reflect upon what other rituals can enhance your inner and outer life.

How can I continually add nurturing aesthetics to my home?
Identify what you have that is your mainstay—the nurturing backbone for your home. As you change or expand your self-growth horizons, your home should respond (with your help). Think about your senses of sight, sound, touch, taste, and smell. You can consider how each adds to the

nuance of your comfort. Even a lovely space can be made brighter with plants or a bowl of fresh fruit. Keeping a little dish of palo santo sticks on the coffee table reminds me that I can easily cleanse my space of negative energy.

How can I bring nature inside?

Streaming sunlight, a breeze from an open window, and the scent of fresh flowers all bring an uplifting liveliness indoors. Your mood may shift with the sound of a torrential rain or the view of a beautiful eucalyptus tree. Pay attention to how your home connects to the outdoors. With intentionality, you can add even more resonance for your well-being.

How does nurturing others also nurture me?

In the midst of a hectic morning or when dashing around to make dinner, I find that pausing even for a few minutes to care for my herbs in the planter box or to pet my dog is a needed respite. I breathe more deeply and I return to my other tasks more relaxed.

My home and I
are in constant
conversation.

Self-Care Rituals

I am committed to making time for myself and being more present. For me to be the best version of myself at work, with my loved ones, and for my daughter requires self-care. While I can always take a hike or attend a Pilates class, it's *within* my home that I need a reliable routine.

From the time you wake up each morning to the time you turn in every night, embrace rituals that enhance how you feel in your home environment and out in the world. What new habit might make you more of a morning person? At night, could you trade in scrolling through Instagram for a luxurious hot bath? These experiences in your personal space strengthen the core of inner calm that needs attention.

In the Morning
This is "get ready" time: Adopt a habit that helps you feel balanced and ready to go. Your home sets the stage for personal transitions and makes your lifestyle possible. Ensure you set yourself up for a successful and enjoyable day through morning routines.

Set your own alarm
As you close your eyes at night, decide what time you want to wake up the next day. Visualize a clock at midnight and then keep moving the arms around through each hour until they land on the time you want to wake up. This exercise takes less than a minute. Set your actual alarm as a backup, but I find that this "internal clock" process usually works. It's a way I stay in tune with myself and harness the power of my mind and natural intuition. The morning light coming in helps, too.

Morning meditation

Whether it's a guided experience through an app or simply sitting still and breathing with awareness for twenty minutes, this daily habit can provide calm and spark creativity that lasts all day. Science confirms that it allows your brain to rest and refocus. Creating an enjoyable ritual around meditation makes you look forward to the daily respite: Light some incense, have a cup of tea, sit on your made bed, or create a designated meditation corner with a cushion and candles.

Breakfast dedication

Replace rushed mornings with a purposeful time to fuel up and to prepare your body and mind for what's to come. You can even get breakfast ready the night before. Set your table with whatever makes it inviting—I arrange a napkin, spoon or fork, and a small bud vase. In the kitchen, I lay out the nonrefrigerated items I need, even premeasuring rolled oats, so it's quick to assemble. Making smart choices for breakfast keeps me on track the whole day. My favorites: oatmeal cooked with a slice of ginger and chia seeds, topped with almond milk and nuts; breakfast tacos with leftover veggies, scrambled eggs, and avocado; or sometimes it's just a cup of miso broth with tofu and chopped greens to replace coffee! Sit down, chew slowly, and nourish yourself.

During the Day

Take breaks to reset, relax, or recharge meaningfully. Whether you're working or lounging, lean on your home to help you have a varied, productive, or chill time. Locate different spots to energize and get a new perspective.

Move your body

Track your day. How much time do you spend sitting, whether at the computer, in the car or subway, watching TV, or texting? We know that being sedentary can reverse the benefits of exercise. So get moving! Take breaks to move every forty minutes, no matter where you are. At home, keep a basket of exercise equipment—a set of weights, a band, and a jump rope—next to a yoga mat. Take a short walk or do some stretching. Even light physical movement is a mood lifter, and will ultimately boost your energy level. You may forgo the 3 P.M. latte you used to need.

Step outside

You'll appreciate your home more if you step outside of it. If you have a balcony, porch, backyard, or rooftop, you can do this often. If you don't, it's still worth making the effort. When weather permits, sit outside with your laptop or with friends on a bench or blanket. Catch a spring breeze or take your shoes off to feel the grass with your bare feet. Connecting with the outdoors helps you slow down, feel more grounded (literally), and recharge your batteries.

In the Evening

Oh, the many ways to enjoy home in the evening. Indulge your senses in the place that is most uniquely you. This is the time for a good meal, wonderful conversations, or a beloved book. Choose unwinding rituals that bring your day to a thoughtful conclusion and set you up for a good night's sleep.

Take a bath or shower

Soaking in water is the best. Submersion has the benefit of heat (improves circulation), pressure against your body (improves blood flow), and buoyancy (lightens the load on your mind). Use salts or bath oil to make it extra luxe—you can even light a favorite candle. If you prefer a shower, hang a bundle of eucalyptus just below your showerhead; the steam releases a heavenly scent for a restful night's sleep. Just five minutes in a warm or hot shower lifts your mood, relaxes your body, eases pain or inflammation, and helps you get to sleep faster. A cold rinse is a "wake up" experience that energizes, improves circulation, and strengthens your immunity by increasing your metabolic rate.

Enhance your zzzs

Lavender is an herb known for calming and promoting sleep. Before you turn in, spritz your bedding with a natural lavender spray—make your own using ten drops of lavender essential oil mixed with two tablespoons rubbing alcohol and six tablespoons of distilled water. Relax into a soothing slumber on your scented sheets.

Breathe before bed

The breath-mind connection is powerful. Scientists have identified links between respiratory patterns and emotions, meaning you can literally use your breath to regulate your state of mind. Breathing helps slow your heart rate, which can lower anxiety, bring peace, and help you rest well. Try this breathing exercise when sleep eludes you.

1. Exhale fully through your mouth.
2. Inhale through your nose for four counts. The pace at which you count is up to you; don't rush.
3. Hold in your breath for seven counts. Set a reasonable pace.
4. Now, take eight full counts to breathe out through your mouth. Go ahead and exhale with some force, feeling the air move past your lips.

Repeat until you fall asleep. This pattern will quickly become natural; you won't even have to count, you can just b-r-e-a-t-h-e.

Scents and Sounds

Scents and sounds evoke mood and memory, and can create a sense of calm or stimulate energy. Think of these less-than-tangible sensations as the final topping of icing on your nurturing home.

Choosing Your Preferred Scents

Scents are about as personal as you can get; you probably know what you like immediately. You may enjoy exploring the variety of natural scents, and the diverse ways they can spice up your space. In my home, you will find soy-based **candles** and an aromatherapy **diffuser** with essential oils alongside my sage and **palo santo sticks**. **Incense, herbs** (both fresh and dried), and **potpourri** and **sachets**—purchased or homemade—are other great sources as well. I have a few recommendations as you delve into this enchanting world.

Go natural

Scents found in nature are more subtle and universally pleasing than heavier, manufactured perfumes.

Use what you have around you

A fragrant posy of rosemary or a small vase of lilies from your garden can have as much impact as anything you buy.

Less is more

Like with seasoning in a recipe, it's better to go light on a scent and add more as needed. It's harder to dial back a fragrance if you go too far.

Consider private versus public spaces

While you might love a combo of rich amber and tobacco, your guests may not. Keep your more specific or robust scents where you'll enjoy them.

Space ratio

A larger candle or intense incense is better in an open space than in a small bath or bedroom where it could overwhelm.

Seeking a specific scent vibe?

These nourish, replenish, and bring in good energy:

Lavender, bergamot, and ylang-ylang encourage sleep

Peppermint, citrus, and eucalyptus stimulate and energize

Sandalwood, rosemary, and vanilla evoke happiness

Music Makes the Mood

Music fills your home in more ways than one. It's not just sound; it also sets a mood or tells a story. It can relax or energize, get a party started or wind a night down. It's deeply personal, but also a shared experience.

So how do you choose the music for the moment? Most of us have our defaults—jazzy tunes for getting dinner ready, a mix of soul and funk for cocktails with friends, or Top 40 to sing along to while straightening up. I add songs that I hear when I'm out and about or in the car to playlists, and ask friends for recommendations to find something new. My music palette is always in flux—just like my mood. Here are a few favorites.

Getting dinner ready: "Dancing in the Moonlight," King Harvest
Cleaning or getting party-ready: "I Wanna Dance with Somebody (Who Loves Me)," Whitney Houston
Relaxing on the couch: "#9 Dream," John Lennon
Just because: "O-o-h Child," Nina Simone
Welcoming friends over: "You Are the Best Thing," Ray LaMontagne
Anytime hanging: "Our House," Crosby, Stills, Nash & Young

Let the Music Play!
Beyond the music you select and play, the way you listen to it can run the gamut from shuffling your playlist to an old-school record collection. Each might be right for a different time and place in your home.

Most Hands-On: Turntable and records
Find a vintage or new turntable, hook up speakers, and shop for some vinyl. A record collection can be interactive: Guests will flip through and engage in conversation while they select their favorites to play.

Curated Set List: Preloaded playlists

Apps allow you to build your own playlists or stream music curated by friends, DJs, radio stations, and musicians. This approach eliminates stress, so you can be in the moment and enjoy.

Hands Off DJing: Job share

Let a designated friend or two take control of the music for the night. You get to be the audience and purely enjoy.

It's Only Natural

In every room, you can add a touch that literally offers a breath of fresh air along with living colors that resonate with the space—and in so doing, elevate your spirit. One of the ways I make an extra effort to care for myself is by bringing home potted plants and flowers from the farmers market. These are part of my essentials. A living thing, whether an olive tree, cactus, or bouquet, can have a presence and power as significant as a sofa or a lamp.

Plants contribute color, shape, and texture, and soften architectural lines in your rooms while offering added dimension. Their benefits go beyond the aesthetic, though. They are natural air purifiers: They clean the air we breathe by eliminating toxins that accumulate when it's stagnant. They also absorb carbon dioxide and release oxygen, giving us more air to breathe. Studies have proven that they can help prevent you from getting sick, and if you are sick, they can help you recover faster.

So plants take care of us, but caring for *them* can be therapeutic as well. Each day, check in with your plants, taking a minute to monitor their signs of growth and general well-being. Pause a bit longer whenever possible to appreciate the beauty they add, breathing deeply in a gentle morning or midday meditation. Acknowledge gratitude for their life and yours.

Pick Your Plant Style

Your perfect plant is about more than your personal preferences. There are many considerations in finding what really works and thrives in and around your home. But selecting something just because it makes you happy is always fine, too!

When I was choosing plants for my indoor and outdoor spaces, I found a nearby nursery with people who were delighted to offer me guidance. They had someone come do a walk-through of my space, and truly collaborated with me so I could bring home what worked best and looked just right—and that I could care for properly, given my daily schedule. Afterward, when I had questions, they were attuned to my needs, and years later, my plants are still thriving. Learning about plants took time, but now I have my favorites for my home, my office, and for gifts. I think of them in these categories.

Umbrella tree

Easy Care

Air plant, cactus, Chinese money plant, dieffenbachia, Guiana chestnut, mother-in-law's tongue, peacock plant, pothos, umbrella tree

Monstera

Striking Shapes

Aloe, black aralia, calathea, jade jewel plant, monstera, palm trees, ponytail palm, snake plant, staghorn fern, succulents, Vriesea, yucca

maidenhair fern

Textural Treats

Asparagus fern, fatsia, iron-cross begonia, maidenhair fern, 'Moon Valley' friendship plant, nerve plant, prayer plant, strawberry begonia, string of pearls

Parlor palm

Space Fillers

Banana tree, bird of paradise, cast-iron plant, fiddle leaf fig, lemon tree, parlor palm, rubber plant, split-leaf philodendron, weeping fig

Natural light matters since plants need sunlight to survive. Do your research up front to see where your home falls on the light spectrum. You can find plants for both sunny and darker rooms.

Space is also a must since plants grow. Read up on the mature height and width for any larger plants and trees you have in mind. Check into what is needed to replant them, and whether a larger plant could do well on a balcony or in a backyard.

Time is another consideration. Different species have a range of maintenance needs; be honest with yourself about what is manageable. A maidenhair fern is stunning and delicate, but it requires daily attention. If you've got minimal time to foster your green thumb, start with an easy-care spider plant and work up to fussier varieties.

Vessels

If you're wondering, "Do I even need a planter?" the answer is yes. Like the plants, the pots and planters you select add style.

TIP If your pot or planter does not have a drainage hole (essential for proper plant care), you can line the bottom with lava rocks to allow for drainage.

A **curvy ceramic pot** lends a bit of polish and feels like a sculpture, while a **textured stone planter** brings a touch of the outdoors inside. Oversized **woven baskets** are a great choice for larger trees. And a **sleek white or black planter** acts as an artful frame for a dramatic plant without taking away from its beauty. To create a mini greenhouse vibe, cluster a few plants in **old-school terra-cotta pots.**

In Bloom

Flowers are an affordable luxury you can pick up anytime to change the mood instantly. They make us feel brighter.

One of these days I plan to take a class on flower arranging. In addition to my desire to learn how to combine and style bouquets, I find it calming to be around and handle flowers. The colors, the variety, and the scents all add up to a pleasurable experience with a

lovely takeaway. In the meantime, I use these easy ideas to make my arrangements look fantastic.

Know your **sources.** Check if the flowers were grown locally or if they have traveled across an ocean to arrive at your shop. Choosing locally grown flowers when possible is good for the environment—and they're likely to hold up better, too.

Choose one flower type or color. It's easy to arrange flowers if you choose one color or a similar palette. Keep in mind that one type of stem en masse never fails to look pleasing to the eye. This route is great for beginners. **Or choose a variety of flowers.** Do something unexpected. Let your inner playfulness come out with a mix of colors and heights, just for the fun of it. If you like a more composed look, **use a rubber band or floral foam to create a tight, neat arrangement.** Be sure the vessel will hide the band.

Vary the vessel. If you don't have a vase on hand, scout your home for **unexpected containers** like an empty candle jar, a shallow bowl, or even a cocktail shaker.

Set your flowers up for success. Cut each stem at an angle when you bring the flowers home. Regular scissors will crush your flower stems; use a **knife or floral shears** instead.

Care for them daily. Be sure to change the water frequently. As flowers wilt, remove the ones that are past their prime and rearrange the rest. Sometimes I end up with nothing but leaves, which also bring life to a counter or table.

Pet Projects

My dog, Lox, is a limitless source of joy, comfort, and companionship. Every time I come home and she bounds over to me in excitement, I am in love all over again. Pets can be a calming and reassuring force in any home. Studies have shown that pet owners have less stress and anxiety and, dogs in particular, promote exercise. They even help us socialize and meet people. Caring for Lox gives me a sense of purpose.

Of course, as much as I love her, I also know it can be challenging to integrate pets thoughtfully into your space. They have their own personalities, moods, and needs. When Lox first came to live with us, I had so much fun setting up a little tepee in the corner of our living room with her special blanket. And she used it regularly! It fulfilled me to know that as much as I had my own special spots throughout the house, she had her own, too. How do you make a house a dog home?

Sleeping
Like you, your four-legged friend wants a cozy place. Choose a pet bed—be sure you have one in the rooms where you spend the most time. Choose a natural fabric covering that looks good in your space; you could even use this opportunity to add a touch of color.

Playtime
Stow pet toys and treats in bins and baskets that fit into a corner or are easily tucked away.

Dining space
Lox's only presence in our kitchen is her two bowls. Up the style factor by finding bowls that suit your home's decor.

8

YOU'RE INVITED

If you love to host, a prepared home and relaxed attitude
make all the difference. An open, welcoming home is
a true expression of caring, and builds community—
whether for an hour, an evening, or a weekend.

My favorite days and nights are those spent at home surrounded by my friends and family. I feel at ease hosting and bringing people together. When I see others relaxing and laughing and connecting, I am happy. It's pretty simple. This is quality time for me, with memories that linger after everyone leaves. My home is a point of pride and for this I am most grateful.

Occasionally I hear friends say they would love to entertain but having guests stresses them out. I get it; I used to feel that way, too. But my desire to have people over mattered more, so I dove in and hosted all kinds of gatherings, from a small, casual dinner to a splashy Fourth of July BBQ. But something wasn't working for me. I realized after my guests left that I hadn't spoken with anyone and had hardly sat down. I enjoyed the idea more than the actual experience. Others were having fun, and I wanted in! What needed to change?

I've learned that doing as much as I can ahead of time is key. And while I do enjoy the busy part of hosting—both before and during (after, with cleanup, not so much)—I realized my friends could help. My best advice is to throw perfection out the window—we all need realistic expectations.

How Does Sharing Your Space
Make a House a Home?

Welcoming guests is one more way your home expresses who you are and what you want to say. Entertaining elevates your awareness of the flow, the styling, and the organization of your home. It's a way to pause and check in with the defining elements, making sure they suit you and the atmosphere you want for your guests.

For me, sharing my home marries two of my favorite things: spending time with friends and creating a particular environment. I enjoy setting the tone—making the choice to keep wine on the counter versus having a bartender, for example. And I have fun with the thematic decorations— how else could you send people to an island luau in the dead of winter? Ask yourself these questions to get an idea about your preferred entertaining style:

What kind of host am I?
Looking at your natural routines and habits will help you decide what type of entertaining best suits you. Like to sleep in? Skip the brunch. If you enjoy everyone pitching in, a potluck may be the way to start. If you want to show off a new seating arrangement on the terrace or patio, have a happy hour. If cornhole is your jam, set up a backyard barbeque. If you are satisfied with having everyone mingle, you're a different host from one who plans games and getting-to-know-you conversations. Try out various approaches that let you explore all the ways your home can help you host.

What type of gathering is my home best suited for?
Think of a checklist of considerations: How many people will your space comfortably hold? Does the weather or season matter in the space

you want to use? How will people gather in different seating areas with appetizers and drinks? Assessing the possibilities and limitations will help you focus on what you can and can't do. My small interior and larger backyard make my home best suited for an afternoon brunch or an al fresco dinner party on a warm summer night.

How much work is right for me right now?

Sometimes you have the bandwidth for a large blowout to celebrate a friend's milestone birthday. Other times, being a minimalist seems like a lot. Balance what you have to do in your life with what you want to do, and know that you can invest more another time if you want to. A low-maintenance after-work cocktail party may be a fit with a few bottles of wine and simple store-bought snacks, plus a preset cue for when it's over. The next weekend may be ideal for that lingering weekend brunch followed by an afternoon sun session.

TIP Be prepared for the unexpected. I keep a bin in my garage labeled "Party!" with the basics for any casual, last-minute gathering. Have an ice bucket and several large trays in your pantry so you are always ready for friends.

The Approach

When you break down the elements of entertaining and sharing your home, you will find an approach that's manageable, and you can plan with confidence. Having people over is for *you* as much as it is for your guests, so keep that idea at the heart of all your choices. You are welcoming people into the haven you've created—you're welcoming them home, too.

Act Natural

I am most comfortable barefoot, so a formal dinner is not my go-to. Whether your natural is great takeout, game night, or bringing in a personal chef, go for it. There are as many ways to host people as there are personalities. Embrace your own style, then try new ideas for fun.

How your home can help: Use the spaces you want to show off and have created to be guest friendly. If you absolutely love your kitchen, have a pizza- or sushi-making party. Proud of your great outdoors? Porch cocktails may be your calling.

Roll with It

Plan as best you can, and know things will follow their own course. You can't control everything. Not everyone will show up on time—let that be okay. If a main course gets burnt, order in Thai. If and when something goes awry, be comfortable with it. Your guests will follow suit. When being together is the priority, everything else falls into place.

How your home can help: If you have a stocked bar cart, ask your guests to invent a house cocktail while you deal with whatever has happened. Setting out nuts and olives in bowls and stacking some great books to peruse will keep guests distracted and entertained. Pump up the music and get the party going!

Keep It Simple

Your friends and family aren't coming over for a five-star chef's tasting menu experience. They are coming to enjoy your company and your home. So instead of overreaching with a complex, time-consuming recipe, make a dish you know and can make well, even if that means a big bowl of spaghetti or burgers on the grill. Remember, a pitcher of iced tea or a few bottles of good wine goes with everything.

How your home can help: Use what you have. A simple cake stand piled with fresh figs and grapes is a tasteful centerpiece. Rather than renting chairs, pull in a mix from your other rooms. The effect is more charming and welcoming than a catering company look.

Forgo All Rules

If you don't have a formal dining area, cushions around a coffee table filled with tea lights is enchanting. If you aren't a cook, host friends for drinks and have everyone bring a favorite appetizer.

How your home can help: Let your home provide inspiration for your gatherings. If you have been collecting glassware on your travels, a wine tasting party is a great way to show it off. Still dreaming about a memorable dinner under the stars in Morocco? Re-create it in your backyard with layers of rugs and your collection of candlesticks.

TIP Make a checklist a few days ahead to stay organized and calm. In the moment, you will have things to do—let others pitch in. Entertaining does not have to be a solo performance. Then you, too, can enjoy the company of your guests, which is why you wanted to have them over in the first place.

My best advice
is to throw
perfection out
the window—we
all need realistic
expectations.

Stay for a While

Welcoming guests to stay overnight should give you a feeling of warmth, not worry. Pull together these basics and little extras so you feel prepared for company. Having things in place ensures that you are a stress-free host, and that your guests feel pampered. Everyone will feel at home in your home.

Start with fresh sheets
I like to make sure the bed is made up nicely ahead of time so that as soon as guests arrive, their space is inviting and cozy. Offering pillows with varying firmness and filling options will help people sleep well. During the colder months, I switch to a slightly darker palette and add a cashmere or wool throw or quilt at the end of the bed.

On the nightstand
Set a welcoming surface with a small vase of flowers, classic book or current magazine, alarm clock, reading light, decanter with water, box of tissues, hand cream, and eye mask. What more could anyone need?

Make some room
Clear out a drawer or two and add some extra hangers in the closet so your guests can put their clothes away. Keep a slim luggage rack in the room so they don't have to put their suitcase on the floor.

House information
It's nice to share your Wi-Fi name and password and any other access notes or details on paper so guests aren't overwhelmed. For people new to the area, I keep a list of must-see spots and favorite places to eat, drink, and hang out.

Extra extras

I always leave out an extra phone charger, as I have forgotten mine countless times when I travel. If you can, put out a lint roller and a shallow dish or bowl for jewelry.

In the bath

Always set out more towels than you think they'll need, including bath towels, hand towels, and washcloths. A bathrobe and slippers are a nice touch.

On the vanity

A few toiletries can come to the rescue during a visit: toothbrush, toothpaste, shampoo and conditioner, soap, and razor. A neutral scented candle lends extra warmth as well.

9

MAKE *HOME* WHEREVER YOU GO

With the joy you have created in your home, leaving for a trip can be bittersweet. When you take the highlights with you, the everyday comforts you treasure can wrap you up no matter where you are.

You've set up a home you love. The ambience and flow are inviting, the space is well laid out and organized, and the accents are pleasing to your senses. You have added special touches, both new and those that honor your significant memories. It's quite an accomplishment! Now comes the hard part—leaving it. But being away from home doesn't have to be difficult. Take the warmth of home with you on a plane, to a hotel, or to your friend's guest room.

I have always loved traveling. From family road trips throughout California to my first trip to Asia, where I river rafted through jungles and had my first surf lesson on the beach in Bali. Traveling at a young age taught me to appreciate new cultures, foods, museums, and our natural world. At age five, when being tucked into bed, I asked my mother, "When am I going to have adventures like you?" The quest for adventure endures! Travel inspires my work and satiates my endless curiosity. I am drawn to the colors, the artisans, the music—the sounds, scents, and flavors. And the people, how they come together, celebrate, and express their exuberance for life.

Living in Italy for many months gave me a different home base for travel and let me try on local lifestyles and my beginner Italian. Based in Florence, I fell in love with the art and architecture and breathtaking experiences around every corner. History mixed with the present. This is where I first became infatuated with textiles and crafts, inquiring into how fabrics were manufactured. I was amazed by the care and time spent across generations to create beautiful, quality products. In retrospect, it's clear how these explorations left a deep impression and, ultimately, inspired Parachute.

Today, travel remains a priority. Even when busy with work and family, driving two hours for a lunch in Santa Barbara or taking a short flight to visit friends in Portland, it's deeply satisfying. Travel isn't always about length and distance. The phrase "a change of scenery" endures for a reason!

Whenever I go, key items from home slip into my suitcase or tote. As a child it was a stuffed toy and favorite sneakers. Now it's a bathrobe (whenever there is an overnight), photos, a throw, and a selection of teas. And I always have room to bring something back. Now, these trips fill my home with keepsakes and practical items I use daily. I like being reminded of the destination and the journey it took to get there and back.

Pack your bags! I have mine at the ready. Whether it's a day trip to ski in the mountains or a three-week drive through Spain, find your travel muse.

How Can Wherever You Go Feel Like Home?

That gray cashmere throw I've mentioned can also be found around my shoulders on airplanes or when I'm strolling through a chilly San Francisco. My favorite hotels offer options for both scents and sounds—that's why they're my favorites. Meditation and a warm bath work at home and at a lodge. When I have at least a few of these anchors during travel, I am in a better mood and ultimately more productive.

What signature details of your home must go in your suitcase?
For the airplane, I have my throw and eye mask. For the hotel room, my bathrobe is a must for personal comfort. A collapsible vase is a recent find that makes adding flowers fun. And I bring a few photographs. Select a few must-haves and pack them before anything else. If something comforts you, make the space to bring it with you.

What's best for a road trip?
Be cautious here. My temptation, and maybe yours, too, is to pack up the whole house inside my car—so be discriminating. In addition to your usual musts, consider adding your comfiest pillow or two, and bringing a cooler for roadside snacks. Maybe toss in some extras, like your own towels. I have books saved in the trunk for an extended vacation. This is also a time to catch up on magazines.

How can homelike elements come to life in my temporary dwelling?
Upon arrival, find a place for all your clothes and toiletries. Use the desk as a workstation so you are ready to be productive. If you meditate, immediately prepare an area.

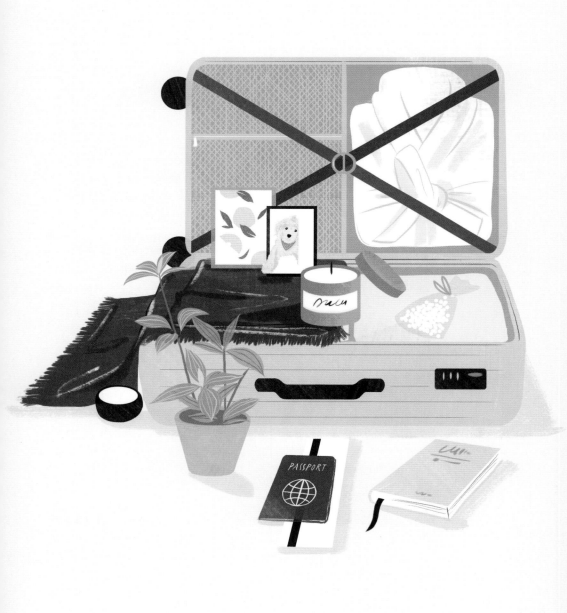

Small Touches

When you travel, you can be minimal yet still include the items that give you maximum comfort. Indulge in a bit of homey luxury. And get packing.

Bring a favorite **candle** in a nonbreakable container to calm your nerves and bring familiarity to foreign spaces. Remember, scents can transport you. And many candles come in travel sizes now.

Pack a **pillowcase** of your own to take along. They take up no space in your suitcase.

A travel-size bottle of **bath oil** will pamper you, but don't stop there. A small bag of **bath salts** and a **lavender sachet** for the drawer are little luxuries you might be craving away from home.

When you arrive, pick up a petite bouquet of **flowers** or a tiny **plant** to add freshness.

Whether you're flying or driving, pack a favorite **tea** or bag of ground **coffee,** so you know you can begin your day as usual. Bring a **reusable water bottle** and a **thermos** for hot beverages.

A **personal photo** in a travel frame or an object that says "home" to you can be a stylish comfort anytime you're on the road.

Live your best life of comfort. When we take time to carry out our intentions, the benefit is all around us. We care for where we are, both at home and as we travel. And in turn, we gain the tangible and intangible benefits of being more at ease in our own skin and our surroundings.

Acknowledgments

Writing a book is never a solo act. I am grateful beyond words for the guidance, the help, the feedback, the humor, the coaxing, the friendship, and the encouragement.

To my editor, Amanda Englander. I am so appreciative you approached me about writing this book. Our first conversation sparked ideas and gave me the confidence to get started and here we are! And to the many others at Clarkson Potter who brought this book to life—thank you Kelli Tokos, Mark McCauslin, Abby Oladipo, Daniel Wikey, Kate Tyler, Jana Branson, Ian Dingman, and Rachel Holzman.

To my agent, Alyssa Reuben at Paradigm Talent Agency. You've helped me navigate this world of writing and publishing with ease. I look forward to what comes next.

To Kerstin Czarra. Thank you for the brainstorms and collaborative sessions to conceptualize and establish the foundation for this book.

To the dream team at Parachute! Thank you for inspiring me every day. Together we are building something that has exceeded my wildest imagination.

To my friends. You lift me up and keep me centered. I am endlessly thankful for our tribe.

To my family. You have shown me the meaning of unconditional love. Thank you for your support, for listening, for being patient, and for always showing up. I am the luckiest.

Index

About the Author

Home is everything to Ariel Kaye, founder and CEO of Parachute. While it began in Los Angeles in 2014 as a digitally native brand, Parachute has since expanded beyond its roots—premium-quality bedding—to include essentials for all rooms in the home. In the last five years, Ariel has evolved Parachute into a beloved home lifestyle brand with numerous brick-and-mortar locations across the country, with each retail store serving as a gathering space within their neighborhoods. Under Ariel's leadership, the brand also launched a hospitality collection, partnering with top hoteliers and interior designers.

Within the Parachute community, Ariel has created a culture committed to wellness and kindness that extends from Parachute's team and partners to its customers and the planet. Social responsibility has been a core tenant of the brand from the start. Parachute partners with the United Nation Foundation's Nothing But Nets campaign to donate one lifesaving malaria-prevention bed net with any one purchase of their signature bedding set.

Parachute has been featured in such notable publications as *The New York Times*, *The Wall Street Journal*, *Domino*, and *Vogue*, while Ariel has participated in prestigious speaking opportunities with *Fortune*'s Most Powerful Women Summit, Create & Cultivate, and *Fast Company*'s Innovation Festival.

Parachute is committed to inspired, comfortable living. Beyond her design and business acumen, Ariel is spearheading a movement around comfort—both in Parachute's stores and for customers around the world.

Ariel currently resides with her family in Venice Beach, California.

Library of Congress Cataloging-in-Publication Data
Names: Kay, Ariel, author. | Lafon, Babeth, illustrator.
Title: How to make a house a home : creating a
    purposeful, personal space / Ariel Kaye ; illustrations
    by Babeth Lafon/Illustration Division.
Description: First edition. | New York : Clarkson
    Potter/Publishers, 2020. | Includes bibliographical
    references and index. | Summary: "How to Make a
    House a Home is more than just a stylish design
    book—Ariel Kaye, the founder of Parachute Home
    (the Madewell of home stores), teaches you how to
    design a home that's not only beautiful, but mindful,
    functional, and nurturing"—Provided by publisher.
Identifiers: LCCN 2019037729 (print) | LCCN
    2019037730 (ebook) | ISBN 9781984826466 | ISBN
    9781984826473 (ebook)
Subjects: LCSH: Interior decoration—Human factors.
Classification: LCC NK2113 .K399 2020 (print) | LCC
    NK2113 (ebook) | DDC 747.7—dc23
LC record available at https://lccn.loc.gov/2019037729
LC ebook record available at https://lccn.loc.
    gov/2019037730

ISBN 978-1-9848-2646-6
Ebook ISBN 978-1-9848-2647-3

Printed in China

Book and cover design by Ian Dingman
Illustrations by Babeth Lafon / Illustration Division

10 9 8 7 6 5 4 3 2 1

First Edition